ACHIEVE LEVEL 5

Grammar, Punctuation and Spelling

Revision and Practice

Louise Moore
Revisions by Maddy Barnes

RISING STARS

CM01583656

PLEASE NOTE: THIS BOOK MAY NOT BE PHOTOCOPIED OR REPRODUCED AND WE APPRECIATE YOUR HELP IN PROTECTING OUR COPYRIGHT.

Rising Stars UK Ltd, 7 Hatchers Mews, Bermondsey Street, London SE1 3GS
www.risingstars-uk.com

Every effort has been made to trace copyright holders and obtain their permission for the use of copyright material. The authors and publishers will gladly receive information enabling them to rectify any error or omission in subsequent editions.

All facts are correct at time of going to press.

© 2012
Published 2012
Reprinted 2012
Reprinted with revisions 2013
New edition printed 2013

Text, design and layout © Rising Stars UK Ltd
Cover design: Burville-Riley Design
Design: David Blundell, Branford Graphics
Layout: Words & Pictures Ltd, London
Editorial: Dawn Booth
Proofreaders: Margaret Crowther and David Mantovani
Illustrations: Phill Burrows (Teachers and Students), p. 56 (top right) iStock / Mike Elliott, p. 56 (top centre) iStock / Kemie, p. 56 (top left) iStock / Ibrahim Sari, p. 56 (bottom right) iStock / dedMazay, p. 56 (bottom left) iStock / Brett Lamb, all others Emily Skinner

All rights reserved. No part of this publication may be reproduced, stored in a retrieval system, or transmitted in any form by any means, electronic, mechanical, photocopying, recording or otherwise, without the prior permission of Rising Stars UK Ltd.

British Library Cataloguing in Publication Data
A CIP record for this book is available from the British Library.

ISBN: 978-0-85769-959-6

Printed by Craftprint International, Singapore

Contents

Answers are in the centre of the book and can be pulled out before handing to the child.

How to use this book

1. Important facts and skills are given at the top of each section. Read them carefully – they show what you really need to know.

2. There is an example question for you to read through. Follow the steps carefully, then try to work through the example yourself.

3. Top tips are given on many pages – they are hints to help you do your best and make learning easier and more fun. Use them well!

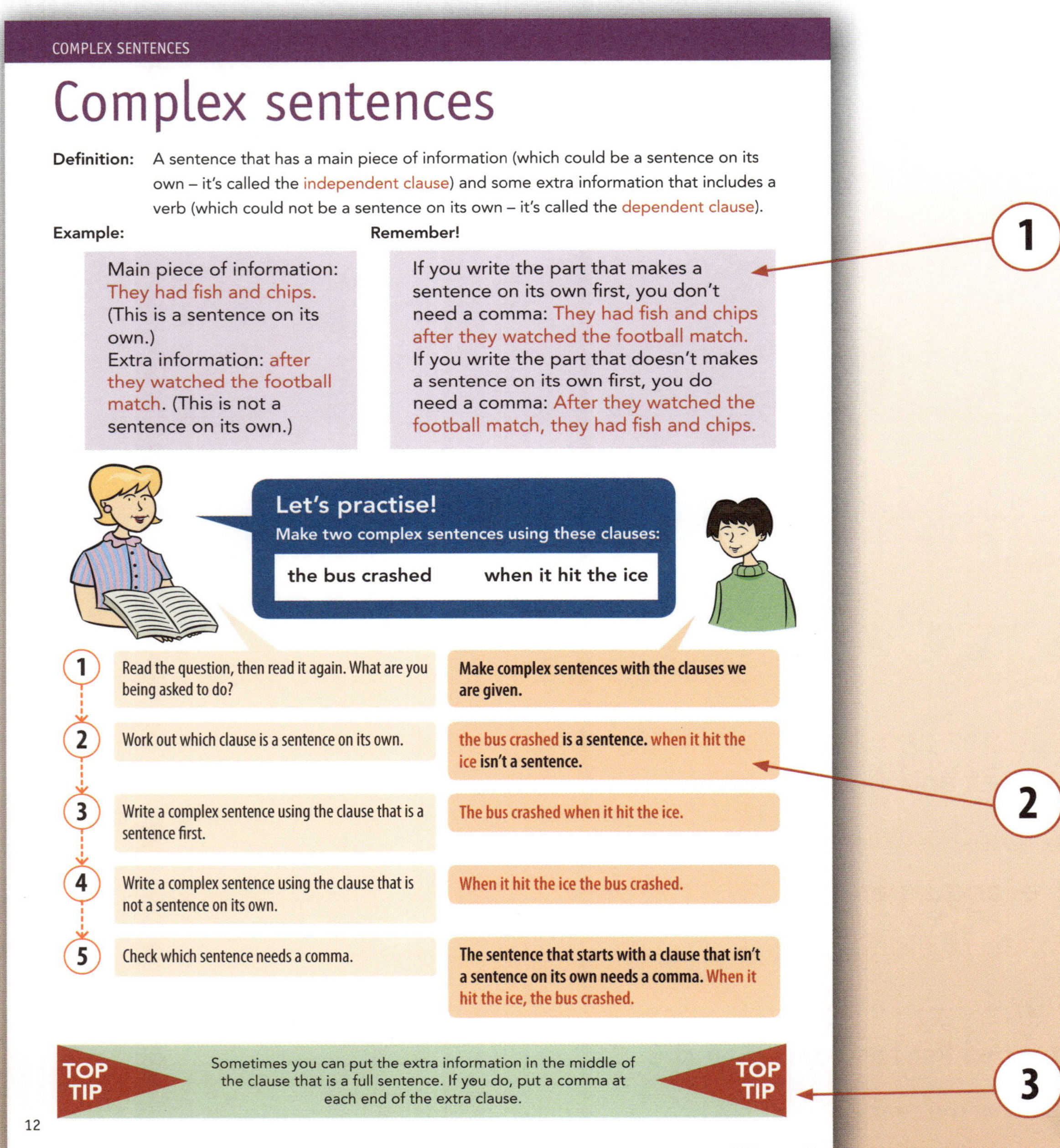

COMPLEX SENTENCES

Complex sentences

Definition: A sentence that has a main piece of information (which could be a sentence on its own – it's called the independent clause) and some extra information that includes a verb (which could not be a sentence on its own – it's called the dependent clause).

Example:

Main piece of information: They had fish and chips. (This is a sentence on its own.)
Extra information: after they watched the football match. (This is not a sentence on its own.)

Remember!

If you write the part that makes a sentence on its own first, you don't need a comma: They had fish and chips after they watched the football match.
If you write the part that doesn't makes a sentence on its own first, you do need a comma: After they watched the football match, they had fish and chips.

Let's practise!

Make two complex sentences using these clauses:

the bus crashed	when it hit the ice

1	Read the question, then read it again. What are you being asked to do?	Make complex sentences with the clauses we are given.
2	Work out which clause is a sentence on its own.	the bus crashed is a sentence. when it hit the ice isn't a sentence.
3	Write a complex sentence using the clause that is a sentence first.	The bus crashed when it hit the ice.
4	Write a complex sentence using the clause that is not a sentence on its own.	When it hit the ice the bus crashed.
5	Check which sentence needs a comma.	The sentence that starts with a clause that isn't a sentence on its own needs a comma. When it hit the ice, the bus crashed.

TOP TIP: Sometimes you can put the extra information in the middle of the clause that is a full sentence. If you do, put a comma at each end of the extra clause.

12

4. Each section has a set of practice questions. Each question has a space for you to write in the answer and a specific number of marks (as in a real National Test). Answers are included in the middle, although your teacher may remove these pages! Marking guidance is provided.

5. Questions are asked in lots of different ways to check that you really understand the topic.

6. If you feel confident with the topic, most sections finish with a challenge. This is a chance to push yourself a little bit further and see what you can achieve!

7. You will see an assessment panel at the top of each set of practice questions. Colour in the face that best describes your understanding of the topic and how you did. Use the spelling list at the end of the book to help you learn and practise your spelling.

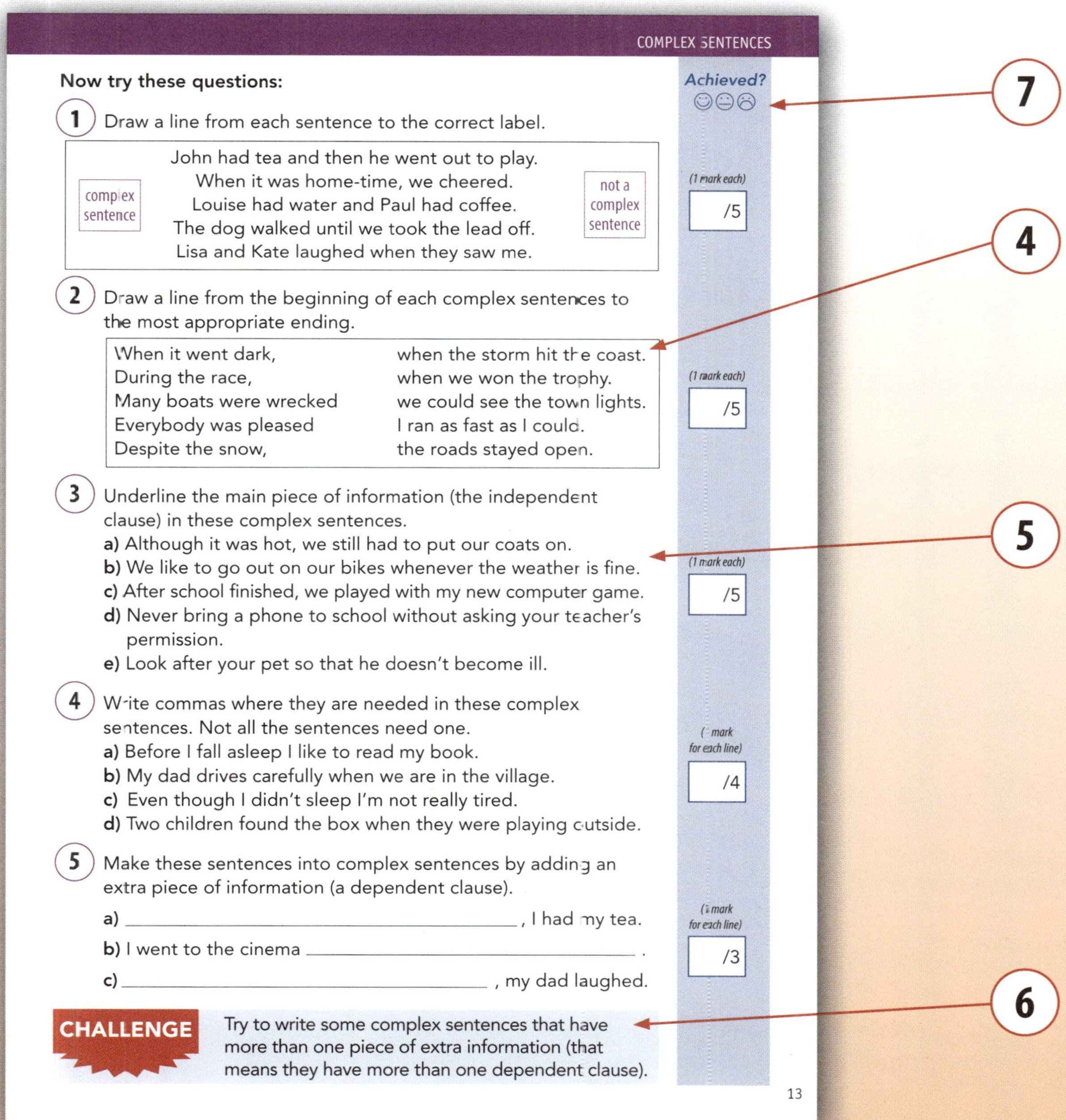
COMPLEX SENTENCES

Now try these questions:

Achieved?

1) Draw a line from each sentence to the correct label.

complex sentence

John had tea and then he went out to play.
When it was home-time, we cheered.
Louise had water and Paul had coffee.
The dog walked until we took the lead off.
Lisa and Kate laughed when they saw me.

not a complex sentence

(1 mark each) /5

2) Draw a line from the beginning of each complex sentences to the most appropriate ending.

When it went dark,	when the storm hit the coast.
During the race,	when we won the trophy.
Many boats were wrecked	we could see the town lights.
Everybody was pleased	I ran as fast as I could.
Despite the snow,	the roads stayed open.

(1 mark each) /5

3) Underline the main piece of information (the independent clause) in these complex sentences.

a) Although it was hot, we still had to put our coats on.
b) We like to go out on our bikes whenever the weather is fine.
c) After school finished, we played with my new computer game.
d) Never bring a phone to school without asking your teacher's permission.
e) Look after your pet so that he doesn't become ill.

(1 mark each) /5

4) Write commas where they are needed in these complex sentences. Not all the sentences need one.

a) Before I fall asleep I like to read my book.
b) My dad drives carefully when we are in the village.
c) Even though I didn't sleep I'm not really tired.
d) Two children found the box when they were playing outside.

(1 mark for each line) /4

5) Make these sentences into complex sentences by adding an extra piece of information (a dependent clause).

a) ______________________, I had my tea.
b) I went to the cinema ______________________.
c) ______________________, my dad laughed.

(1 mark for each line) /3

CHALLENGE Try to write some complex sentences that have more than one piece of extra information (that means they have more than one dependent clause).

13

Revision of word classes

These are the word classes that you should already be familiar with.

Word class	Explanation
Articles	the words a, an or the that come before a noun
Nouns	name a person, animal, place, thing or idea
Pronouns	take the place of a noun in a sentence
Adjectives	describe nouns
Verbs	give an action or happening
Adverbs	give more information about verbs
Conjunctions	connectives used to link different ideas in a sentence
Connectives	link different phrases, sentences and paragraphs together
Prepositions	show the position of things

Let's practise!
Which word classes does the word light belong to?

1	Read the question, then read it again. What are you being asked to do?	**Work out the word classes that the word light could belong to.**
2	Work out the classes that definitely don't contain light.	**It can't be an article, a pronoun, a conjunction or connective.**
3	Could it be a noun?	**Yes – a light is the name of an object.**
4	Could it be an adjective?	**Yes – something could be light to carry.**
5	Could it be a verb?	**Yes – you can light a fire.**
6	Could it be an adverb?	**No – you could run lightly, not light.**
7	Could it be a preposition?	**No – light can't relate two things.**
8	Write your answer.	**Light can be a noun, an adjective or a verb.**

TOP TIP

It is sometimes thought to be poor grammar to end a sentence with a preposition. This won't always be possible, but try to avoid ending sentences with words such as:

at by for on to up upon with

Now try these questions:

Achieved? ☺ 😐 ☹

1 Which word classes can these words belong to?

a) date ______________________ *(2 marks)*

b) hard ______________________ *(2 marks)*

c) rush ______________________ *(3 marks)*

d) prime ______________________ *(3 marks)*

e) coat ______________________ *(2 marks)*

/12

2 Write the correct label in each box:
ART for Article N for Noun V for Verb ADV for Adverb ADJ for Adjective C for Connective P for Preposition PN for Pronoun

Suddenly,	we	saw	a	shape	emerge	from	the	shadows.

The	dogs	howled	because	of	the	fireworks.

Eat	healthy	foods	while	you	are	growing.

Although	it	is	cold,	I	am	going.

(1 mark for every 2 correct)

/15

3 Build sentences using the types of words shown in the boxes.

connective	article	adjective	noun
verb	adverb		

noun	verb	adverb	preposition
article	noun	preposition	noun

article	adjective	noun	verb
connective	pronoun	adverb	verb

(1 mark for every 2 correct)

/11

CHALLENGE

List all the types of each word class that you know and then try to find some more.

Nouns

There are different types of nouns. Have a look at the table and see which of them you recognise.

Type of noun	Explanation	Examples
abstract	name of something that can't be felt or touched	anger, love, honesty, thoughtfulness
collective	name for a group of things	flock, herd, pack, library, swarm
common	name for an ordinary object or animal	cat, table, cup
proper	the name of a particular person, place or thing	Paris, Fred, Brazil, Spanish
uncountable	something that can't be counted, often used with words such as much or a little bit	water, air, life, milk, music

Let's practise!

Match each noun to the correct label.

jealousy	team	French	travel
uncountable noun	abstract noun	collective noun	proper noun

1 Read the question, then read it again. What are you being asked to do?

Decide on the types of noun.

2 Check for the most straightforward noun.

We need a proper noun. It will be the name of something and start with a capital letter. It must be French.

3 Check for the next most straightforward noun.

We need a collective noun. It will be a word that is used for a group of something. It must be team.

4 Check for the next most straightforward noun.

We need an abstract noun. It will be a word that is used for a feeling or quality. It must be jealousy.

5 Check the remaining answer.

Travel – this is a noun that we can't count, so it is an uncountable noun.

jealousy	team	French	travel
uncountable noun	abstract noun	collective noun	proper noun

Now try these questions:

Achieved? ☺ 😐 ☹

1 Write the nouns in the correct boxes. Some words will go in more than one box.

bravery London weather Harry clarinet happiness family art health chair New York advice English curiosity bag Uncle Gary company freedom trust bus army furniture fear electricity audience

Abstract nouns	Collective nouns	Common nouns	Proper nouns	Uncountable nouns

(1 mark for each correct entry) /32

2 Circle all the nouns in these sentences.

a) When Charlotte's anger affected her work, she had to eat chocolate.

b) When a bunch of flowers arrived, Miss Lomas's embarrassment showed.

c) Harvey got the help he needed with his homework from Rio.

d) The greed of some children is a problem for everyone.

e) The school council had an agreement with Mrs Hartley about playground equipment.

(1 mark for each sentence) /5

3 Write the collective nouns for these groups, using your dictionary to help you.

a) ______________ of beauties **b)** ______________ of elephants
c) ______________ of ants **d)** ______________ of geese
e) ______________ of kittens **f)** ______________ of lions
g) ______________ of beavers **h)** ______________ of owls
i) ______________ of crows **j)** ______________ of whales

(1 mark each) /10

4 Write a capital letter at the start of each proper noun in these sentences.

a) My first school was called gleadless primary school.

b) The best book about cats is called the cat kingdom.

c) My favourite uncle is uncle tom.

d) At headless cross there is thought to be a headless ghost.

e) Whaley memorial park is a fantastic park to visit.

(1 mark for each line) /5

CHALLENGE Find all the uncountable nouns you can. Can you think of a way to group the nouns you found?

Expanded noun phrases

Definitions: An expanded noun phrase is a group of words in a sentence that function like a noun.
To create an expanded noun phrase you expand the noun and add extra information.
An expanded noun phrase does not contain a verb, but often includes an article (a, an or the).

Examples:

dog
Expanded noun phrase: The small black dog with white patches
girl
Expanded noun phrase: The beautiful young girl in the park
house
Expanded noun phrase: The haunted house next door to the graveyard
sandwich
Expanded noun phrase: The mouldy sandwich at the bottom of the bag

Let's practise!

Expand the noun into a noun phrase by adding words before and after the noun.

the car

1	Read the question, then read it again. What are you being asked to do?	Add words before and after the noun to create an expanded noun phrase.
2	Check that you know what an expanded noun phrase is.	An expanded noun phrase gives extra information about the noun and does not include any verbs.
3	Think about how you can describe the noun.	You might use adjectives and prepositions.
4	Write the answer.	The red sporty car in the front garden.

Now try these questions:

Achieved? ☺ 😐 ☹

1 Underline the expanded noun phrase in each sentence.

a) The old sensible lady waited at the bus stop.
b) The boy ate the tasty chocolate ice-cream.
c) My teacher gave everybody a scented sticker.
d) Usually I cycle home on my blue mountain bike.
e) I have just finished an amazing comedy novel.

(1 mark each) /5

2 Are these expanded noun phrases accurate? Mark each one and explain the errors. One has been done for you.

the grass is green.	*This is not an expanded noun phrase. Although 'green' is an adjective describing the grass, there is a verb (is) included.*
the cake smelled delicious.	
my annoying little sister	
the angry impatient teacher	
his new sporty green bag was cool	
my heavy bag snapped	

(1 mark each) /5

3 Expand the noun into a noun phrase by adding words before and after the noun.

Noun	**Noun phrase**
the table	
the book	
the elephant	

(1 mark each) /3

Complex sentences

Definition: A sentence that has a main piece of information (which could be a sentence on its own – it's called the independent clause) and some extra information that includes a verb (which could not be a sentence on its own – it's called the dependent clause).

Example:

Main piece of information: They had fish and chips. (This is a sentence on its own.)
Extra information: after they watched the football match. (This is not a sentence on its own.)

Remember!

If you write the part that makes a sentence on its own first, you don't need a comma: They had fish and chips after they watched the football match.
If you write the part that doesn't make a sentence on its own first, you do need a comma: After they watched the football match, they had fish and chips.

Let's practise!

Make two complex sentences using these clauses:

the bus crashed   when it hit the ice

1	Read the question, then read it again. What are you being asked to do?	Make complex sentences with the clauses we are given.
2	Work out which clause is a sentence on its own.	the bus crashed is a sentence. when it hit the ice isn't a sentence.
3	Write a complex sentence using the clause that is a sentence first.	The bus crashed when it hit the ice.
4	Write a complex sentence using the clause that is not a sentence on its own.	When it hit the ice the bus crashed.
5	Check which sentence needs a comma.	The sentence that starts with a clause that isn't a sentence on its own needs a comma. When it hit the ice, the bus crashed.

TOP TIP Sometimes you can put the extra information in the middle of the clause that is a full sentence. If you do, put a comma at each end of the extra clause. **TOP TIP**

Now try these questions:

Achieved? ☺ 😐 ☹

1 Draw a line from each sentence to the correct label.

complex sentence		not a complex sentence
	John had tea and then he went out to play.	
	When it was home-time, we cheered.	
	Louise had water and Paul had coffee.	
	The dog walked until we took the lead off.	
	Lisa and Kate laughed when they saw me.	

(1 mark each) /5

2 Draw a line from the beginning of each complex sentence to the most appropriate ending.

When it went dark,	when the storm hit the coast.
During the race,	when we won the trophy.
Many boats were wrecked	we could see the town lights.
Everybody was pleased	I ran as fast as I could.
Despite the snow,	the roads stayed open.

(1 mark each) /5

3 Underline the main piece of information (the independent clause) in these complex sentences.

a) Although it was hot, we still had to put our coats on.
b) We like to go out on our bikes whenever the weather is fine.
c) After school finished, we played with my new computer game.
d) Never bring a phone to school without asking your teacher's permission.
e) Look after your pet so that he doesn't become ill.

(1 mark each) /5

4 Write commas where they are needed in these complex sentences. Not all the sentences need one.

a) Before I fall asleep I like to read my book.
b) My dad drives carefully when we are in the village.
c) Even though I didn't sleep I'm not really tired.
d) Two children found the box when they were playing outside.

(1 mark for each line) /4

5 Make these sentences into complex sentences by adding an extra piece of information (a dependent clause).

a) ______________________________, I had my tea.

b) I went to the cinema ______________________________.

c) ______________________________, my dad laughed.

(1 mark for each line) /3

CHALLENGE Try to write some complex sentences that have more than one piece of extra information (that means they have more than one dependent clause).

Phrases and clauses

Understanding phrases and clauses helps you to understand punctuation. Punctuation marks, such as commas, semi-colons and colons, are often required with either a phrase or a clause.

Definitions: A **phrase** is a group of words that may have nouns and verbs but does not have a subject doing a verb. For example:

some frightening people　　running down the hill
going to the shops　　after the terrible meal

A **clause** is a group of words that has a subject doing a verb. For example:

he can lift a car　　because she liked picking flowers
when it is time to go home　　Jake plays football

An **independent clause** can be a complete sentence by itself. For example:

He can lift a car.　　Jake plays football.

A **subordinate** (or **dependent**) **clause** starts with a subordinating conjunction and that means it doesn't make sense by itself. For example:

when it is time to go home　　because she liked picking flowers

Let's practise!

Circle any clauses and underline any phrases in this sentence.

Renowned for his sporting prowess, Barti raced to victory at the Winter Championship.

1	Read the question, then read it again. What are you being asked to do?	Circle the clauses and underline the phrases.
2	Split the sentence into sections.	a) Renowned for his sporting prowess, b) Barti raced to victory c) at the Winter Championship.
3	Check if a subject is doing a verb in each section.	a) no; b) yes; c) no
4	If the answer is no, that must be a phrase.	Renowned for his sporting prowess and at the Winter Olympics are phrases.
5	If the answer is yes, that must be a clause.	Barti raced to victory is a clause.
6	Write the answer.	Renowned for his sporting prowess, Barti raced to victory at the Winter Championship.

Now try these questions:

Achieved? ☺ 😐 ☹

1 Write a **P** after a phrase and a **C** after a clause.

(1 mark each) /8

a) the dog barked
b) when they went skating
c) after a long time
d) because it was time
e) the blazing hot sun
f) many people saw the show
g) it rained all day
h) when he saw the parcel

2 Circle the independent clauses and underline the dependent clauses.

(1 mark for each line) /5

a) The dog whined when it heard the fireworks.
b) Because it was snowing, we built a large snowman.
c) We were allowed cake since it was my birthday.
d) Reece fell down so we had to abandon the race.
e) When Louie was away, we did a maths test.

3 Match each group of words to the correct label.

(1 mark each) /8

a large shaggy dog	phrase	clouds form over hills
despite the rain	independent clause	eating his dinner
as he lifted the lid		during the interval
the children were glad	dependent clause	when I go home

4 In these sentences, highlight the phrases, underline the independent clauses and circle the dependent clauses.

(1 mark for each line) /4

a) Whilst watching the match, Sonal started to feel ill.
b) The forest was dark and gloomy; the mountains were light and airy.
c) The phone rang just as tea was ready.
d) When he saw the bill, Sam was very cross.

5 Write an independent clause to complete these sentences.

(1 mark for each line) /3

a) While it was raining, ______________________________ .
b) ______________________ after she finished her homework.
c) ______________________________ because it was hot.

CHALLENGE Take a passage from a book and list all the phrases, dependent clauses and independent clauses. Which list is longest? Why do you think that is?

Embedded clauses

Definitions: Embedded clauses are clauses that are in the middle of a sentence – as if they are tucked up in bed! They are separated from the rest of the sentence, usually by commas.

To make a sentence with an embedded clause:

1 Write a simple sentence: The boy jumped up.

2 Think about some extra information about the boy (perhaps what he looked like or what he was doing apart from jumping up).
He was wearing pyjamas. He was watching a film. He had freckles.

3 Choose the information you are going to use and make it into a clause starting with which or who: who was watching a film

4 Put the clause in the middle of the sentence, with a comma before and after it: The boy, who was watching a film, jumped up.

Let's practise!

Put the commas in this sentence to show the embedded clause.

The door which was the only way out was locked.

1	Read the question, then read it again. What are you being asked to do?	**Put the commas in the sentence to show the embedded clause.**
2	Think what the sentence says.	**It is telling us about the door.**
3	Look at the beginning and end of the sentence to find the simple sentence.	**The beginning says The door and the end tells us it was locked, so the simple sentence is The door was locked.**
4	Look at what else the sentence says.	**It also says which was the only way out so this is the embedded clause.**
5	Put a comma before and after the embedded clause.	**The door, which was the only way out, was locked.**

TOP TIP

Commas can change the meaning of a sentence.
Boys who are energetic like dodgeball.
This tells us that only energetic boys like dodgeball.
Boys, who are energetic, like dodgeball.
This tells us that all boys are energetic and like dodgeball.

TOP TIP

Now try these questions:

Achieved? ☺ 😐 ☹

1 Underline the embedded clause in each of these sentences.

a) The umbrella, which was new, blew inside out.
b) The drink, which was too hot, burned Lani's mouth.
c) Joe, who wasn't holding the handlebars, fell off his bike.
d) The school play, which was superb, was called *Let's Get Away!*
e) Isabella, who was reading, got told off for not listening.

(1 mark each) /5

2 Put the commas in these sentences to show the embedded clauses.

a) The art lesson which lasted for one hour involved modelling.
b) Assemblies which we have every day are too long.
c) Truck drivers who often have to drive all day have to take regular rest breaks.
d) The farmer who needed to harvest his hay watched the weather forecast.
e) Robert who was frightened ran into the house.

(1 mark for each line) /5

3 Tick the sentences that are written correctly. If a sentence is incorrect, explain why.

a) Eleanor who likes, to learn, has a fantastic smile.

____

b) The chair, which was cracked, broke when I sat down.

____

c) These bananas, they are all green, are not ripe.

____

d) Mrs Butcher, best teacher ever, taught us English.

____

e) The children, who were bored, started to throw things.

____

(1 mark for each line) /5

4 Make these simple sentences complex by inserting an embedded clause.

a) The house is old. ______________________________
b) The car is new. ______________________________
c) Children like telling jokes. ______________________________
d) Petrol is very expensive. ______________________________
e) William likes using the robots. ______________________________

(1 mark for each line) /5

CHALLENGE

Write as many sentences with embedded clauses as you can where removing the commas leaves a complete sentence with a different meaning.
Can you see a pattern in your answers?

Active and passive sentences

Definitions: A sentence is **active** when the subject is doing the action (verb). For example:

The police car was following the lorry.

The **subject** is the police car. The **verb** is following. The **object** is the lorry.
The police car is doing the following.

A sentence is **passive** when the subject has the action done to it. For example:

The lorry was being followed by the police car.

The **subject** is the lorry. The **verb** is followed. The **object** is the police car.
The lorry is being followed.

Let's practise!

Change this sentence from the active to the passive voice.

George opened the door.

1	Read the question, then read it again. What are you being asked to do?	**Change the sentence from the active to the passive voice.**
2	Work out what is the subject, what is the object and what is the verb.	**The subject is George. The object is the door. The verb is opened.**
3	Move the object to the position of the subject.	**the door ...**
4	Move the subject to the position of the object and write by before it.	**the door ... by George.**
5	Use the verb to be and change the verb to fit the new sentence.	**It's the past tense so to be will be was or were. The door is singular so you need was.**
6	Write the full sentence.	**The door was opened by George.**

TOP TIP

Sentences in the active voice are easier to read and understand, so it is generally better to use the active voice.

Use the passive voice:
- when the person doing the action is unknown
- if you don't want to say who did the action
- for variety.

TOP TIP

Now try these questions:

Achieved? ☺ 😐 ☹

1 Join each sentence to the correct label. *(1 mark each)* /6

Andy was interested in sport.	active sentence	The class was taught by Mrs Butcher.
The bus was hit by a car.		Caitlin won the race.
The man was arrested by the police.	passive sentence	Vikki was tested by Mrs Sellars.

2 Write **A** after the sentences that are active and **P** after the sentences that are passive. *(1 mark each)* /4

a) The sheep was chased by the dog.
b) A shoal of fish swam underneath the boat.
c) The table was bought by Mr Pattison.
d) The students protested about the lack of aid to Africa.

3 Change these passive sentences to active sentences. *(1 mark for each line)* /4

a) The cake had been eaten by the children.

____

b) The game was being spoiled by the infants.

____

c) The play was appreciated by the audience.

____

d) The plants are hidden by the snow.

____

4 Change these active sentences to passive sentences. *(1 mark for each line)* /3

a) James is chasing after Harvey.

____

b) Megan is laughing at Skye.

____

c) Mrs Mellor is helping Ms Wright.

____

CHALLENGE

1 Count all the passive sentences you can find in two pages of a book. Why do you think there are that many?

2 Find some passive sentences in a reading book and change them to active sentences.

Subject, object and verb

Definitions: To understand sentences, it is helpful to be able to identify the basic units (main parts). These are the subject, object and verb (sometimes called the predicate).

	What it is	About it
subject	the person or thing doing the action	agrees with the verb
object	the person or thing affected by or receiving the action	does not affect the verb
verb	the action being done	known as the predicate

To check if a noun is the subject or object use this simple test:

1 Change the verb to the simple present tense (or a continuous form using –ing, for example: working).
2 Change the noun from singular to plural (or vice versa) and check if you need to change the verb.
3 If the answer is yes, then the noun you changed is the subject.
If the answer is no, then the noun you changed is the object.

Let's practise!

Find the subject, object and verb in this sentence.

The children in the class determined the arrangement of the tables.

1	Read the question, then read it again. What are you being asked to do?	**Find the subject, object and verb (also known as the predicate).**
2	What is the verb?	**The thing being done is determined.**
3	Is the subject easy to identify?	**No. It could be children or tables.**
4	Check the form of the verb.	**It is in the past tense, so change it to the present: I determine, he determines, they determine. The children in the class determine the arrangement of the tables. the table: The children in the class determine the arrangement of the table. This doesn't affect the verb. the child: The child in the class determines the arrangement of the tables. This affects the verb so children is the subject.**
5	Test the subject by changing the nouns to singulars and checking if they change the verb.	**subject – the children verb – determined object – the tables**

Now try these questions:

Achieved? ☺ 😐 ☹

1 Underline the subject and highlight the verb (predicate) in each of these sentences.

a) The owl hoots.
b) A lady screamed.
c) The children were skipping.
d) The bus stopped.
e) They are busy.
f) The fire-engine is red.

(1 mark for each line) /6

2 Complete the table.

Sentence	Subject	Object	Verb
The man washed the car.			
The trees were uprooted by the wind.			
Over the sea, the ship was sailing.			
The traffic jam went through Manchester.			
Across the lawn danced the fairies.			

(1 mark for each cell) /15

3 Identify the word in bold as the subject or object of each sentence.

a) Caitlin hammered the **pegs** into the ground. ____________
b) Before bedtime, **Joshua** had read his magazine. ____________
c) Running quickly, Lucy just managed to catch the **train**. ____________
d) When it is sunny, **he** walks home. ____________
e) The **stone**, which had been thrown by Eleanor, was very heavy. ____________

(1 mark each) /5

4 Decide whether the subject or the verb is missing and then complete the sentence with a suitable word.

a) ______________________ opened the door.
The subject / verb is missing.

b) John was totally unreliable, ______________________ the cub meeting.
The subject / verb is missing.

c) Even though it was Sunday, ______________________ were too busy to sit and read.
The subject / verb is missing.

(2 marks for each line) /6

CHALLENGE Find out about compound subjects and verbs, explain what they are and write some sentences using them.

Adverbs and adverbials

Definitions: An **adverb** is a type of word (a single word) that describes a verb.

An **adverbial** is part of a sentence that tells us more about the verb (and can be more than one word). An adverb can be an adverbial. For example:

William will finish soon. Soon is an adverb that tells us when William will finish.

William will finish in a few minutes. In a few minutes is an adverbial that tells us when William will finish.

Both sentences give us similar information. Adverbials answer questions like:

	Examples
Where?	Tom hid the box under the stairs.
When?	Tom hid the box before breakfast.
How long?	Tom hid the box for a week.
How often?	Tom hid the box every day.
How?	Tom hid the box by covering it with coats.
Why?	Tom hid the box so Jackie wouldn't find it.
With whom?	Tom hid the box with Joe.

Let's practise!

Underline the verb and circle the adverbial in this sentence.

Alli ran as far as the station.

1	Read the question, then read it again. What are you being asked to do?	Underline the verb and circle the adverbial.
2	Find the verb and circle it.	Alli ran – so ran is the verb.
3	What are you told about how she ran?	We are told where she ran – as far as the station. The adverbial is as far as the station.
4	Underline the verb and circle the adverbial.	Alli ran as far as the station.

TOP TIPS

1 Adverbials give the reader more information. Think about extra information that would interest your audience.

2 If an adverbial starts the sentence, it is followed by a comma.

TOP TIPS

Now try these questions:

Achieved? ☺ 😐 ☹

1 Circle the verbs and underline the adverbials in these sentences.

a) Jane sat with her legs crossed.
b) The fan worked to cool the air.
c) After the meal, Sam slept.
d) When it rained, the children ran inside.
e) Molly knocked because she wanted to come in.

(1 mark for each line) /5

2 Write **where? when? how long? how often? how? why?** or **with whom?** after each sentence to show the question each adverbial answers.

a) The plants died because there was a drought. __________
b) Kali worked for three hours. __________
c) Isidore whistled through his front teeth. __________
d) A tree grew on the mountainside. __________
e) Before the holiday, they had to pack. __________
f) Every week, Aiden went to Scouts. __________

(1 mark each) /6

3 Write each sentence adding an adverbial that answers the question at the end.

a) The cat purred. **Why?** __________
b) The building collapsed. **When?** __________
c) Lucy Mae practised the piano. **How often?**
____
d) Barti went to the park. **With whom?**
____
e) Renata worked. **How?** __________

(1 mark for each line) /5

4 Write a sentence containing each adverbial. Make sure that the adverbial is telling you more about the verb.

a) at the weekend __________
b) by the canal __________
c) every three hours __________
d) to check how well we were doing
____
e) for a fortnight __________

(1 mark for each line) /5

CHALLENGE Try using connectives to start adverbials. How many different connectives can you find that will work?

Connectives and cohesion

Definitions: **Connectives** link together ideas in one sentence or between different sentences and paragraphs.
Linking ideas and sentences gives your writing **cohesion** – it holds it together and gives it more meaning.

Connectives can be grouped into different types, according to their function in the sentence. Look at the types and the example given for each:

Qualifying connectives although	Illustrating connectives such as	Contrasting connectives alternatively	Adding connectives also
Comparing connectives likewise	Cause and effect connectives so	Emphasising connectives in particular	Sequencing connectives finally

Let's practise!

Choose suitable connectives to join these sentences. You may want to change some of the words and word orders.

a) The boys teased the girls. They got into trouble.
b) Jake likes cars. He likes Ferraris the best.

1. Read the question, then read it again. What are you being asked to do?
   Link the sentences using connectives.
2. How are the first two sentences connected?
   The second sentence is caused by what happens in the first sentence.
3. Select a suitable cause and effect connective.
   consequently links the two sentences: The boys teased the girls. Consequently, they got into trouble.
4. How are the second two sentences connected?
   The second sentence emphasises the first sentence.
5. Select a suitable emphasising connective.
   especially links the two sentences: Jake likes cars, especially the Ferraris.

• BEWARE • BEWARE • BEWARE • BEWARE • BEWARE •

Not all connectives are conjunctions. If they are not conjunctions, they need to be used in a new sentence or with a conjunction in the same sentence. Especially acts as a conjunction, but consequently doesn't.

Now try these questions:

Achieved?

1 **a)** Write each connective in the correct box in the table.

if, moreover, for instance, thus, as well as, otherwise, like, eventually, for example, first, consequently, as revealed by, indeed, equally, and, before, as with, significantly, despite, in the case of, next, therefore, as long as, after, similarly, whereas, meanwhile, since, above all, instead of, in the same way, unlike, unless, notably, because, too, then, especially, however, except

Qualifying connectives although	**Illustrating connectives** such as	**Contrasting connectives** alternatively	**Adding connectives** also
Comparing connectives likewise	**Cause and effect connectives** so	**Emphasising connectives** in particular	**Sequencing connectives** finally

(1 mark for every 2 in boxes and 1 mark for every 2 highlighted)

/33

b) Highlight the connectives in the table that could be used as conjunctions.

2 Make the most suitable matches between the different parts of the sentence.

First part of the sentence	**Connectives with conjunctions**	**Second part of the sentence**
I peeled the vegetables	so, consequently,	Max lit the fire.
I was late	and, meanwhile,	someone answered the door.
I kept pressing the bell	until, eventually,	I missed the bus.
Everyone went on the trip	as well as	today was his birthday.
I did the shopping	especially as	cleaning the house.
I finished my work	except	lunchtime.
William was happy,	during	the boys who broke the window.

(1 mark for each line)

/7

CHALLENGE Write a paragraph using a variety of connectives to give your writing cohesion.

Impersonal writing

Definition: Impersonal writing avoids personal pronouns (I, he, she, we, you, our, us).
Impersonal writing avoids using emotional words to influence the reader.

Examples:

Personal writing	Impersonal writing
I think the way the bears are treated is criminal.	The bears are kept in poor conditions.
Lots of people know that the tests are far too hard for children like us.	It is generally believed that the tests are too hard.
We all thought that lunch was disgusting.	There were problems with the lunch.

Let's practise!

Change this sentence to make it impersonal.

I thought that the train ride was a total disaster.

1	Read the question, then read it again. What are you being asked to do?	Make the sentence impersonal.
2	Look for the personal pronouns.	I is the personal pronoun used.
3	Write the sentence without the personal pronoun.	Some people thought that the train ride was a total disaster.
4	Look for emotional words.	Total disaster are the emotional words that would influence the reader.
5	Write the sentence without the emotional words.	Some people thought that the train ride was disappointing.
6	Check that the sentence is impersonal.	The sentence still mentions some people. This can be made even more impersonal by writing: It is thought that the train ride was disappointing.

TOP TIP Impersonal writing is used by scientists who want to share their ideas. Impersonal writing makes readers think that they are reading about facts rather than opinions. **TOP TIP**

Now try these questions:

Achieved? ☺ 😐 ☹

1 Circle the words that make these sentences personal.

a) The party made me ecstatic.
b) We all want to stop harmless creatures being tortured.
c) I think I should be allowed to go.
d) You might disagree with me, but that would be a dangerous mistake.
e) If we all take this seriously, I will be delighted.

(1 mark for each line) /5

2 Complete the table by ticking the boxes to show which sentences are personal and which are impersonal.

	Personal writing	Impersonal writing
I know that football teams have to travel a lot.		
Pandas are at risk of extinction.		
Snakes are dangerous creatures that should be avoided		
If I can do this, anybody can.		
It is thought that children have to learn too much.		
Never make the same mistake that I did.		
Dreadful, frightening events are threatening our survival.		

(1 mark for each line) /7

3 Join each sentence to the correct label.

impersonal writing

Most countries have concerns.
Nobody would consider this idea.
Of course, Katy loves ice-cream.
In my opinion, that would be a mistake.

personal writing

(1 mark each) /4

4 Rewrite these sentences making them more impersonal.

a) I know that cars go too fast.

____

b) We think that spiders are brilliant.

____

c) It would be fantastic if we went sailing.

____

d) I know everyone would prefer red shirts.

____

e) I went to check what was happening yesterday.

____

(1 mark for each line) /5

CHALLENGE Write a paragraph using impersonal language. Check that you avoid personal pronouns and check that you don't use emotive words to give away your opinions!

Formal writing and Standard English

Definition: Standard English is English that follows accepted rules of grammar and that many people believe to be 'correct'. It is usual to use Standard English in formal situations.

Some rules to consider:

- Always use complete sentences.
- Try to avoid starting sentences with a conjunction.
- Try to avoid ending sentences with a preposition.
- Make sure tenses are correct.
- Make sure subjects and verbs agree.
- Write in the third person (use one instead of you).
- Avoid double negatives, contractions and abbreviations.
- Avoid idioms, figurative language and colloquialisms (words generally used in informal conversations).
- Use precise and technical language.
- Be as objective as possible.

Let's practise!

Rewrite this sentence using Standard English.

So he'd chucked it out of window 'cos he don't know nobody were under.

1	Read the question, then read it again. What are you being asked to do?	Change the passage to Standard English.
2	Check that the sentence is complete, doesn't start with a conjunction and doesn't end with a preposition.	He'd chucked it out of the window 'cos he didn't know that underneath were nobody.
3	Check the person, tenses and subject–verb agreement.	He'd chucked it out of the window 'cos he didn't know that underneath there was nobody.
4	Remove double negatives, contractions and abbreviations.	He had chucked it out of the window because he did not know that underneath there was somebody.
5	Remove idioms, figurative language and colloquialisms.	He had thrown it out of the window because he did not know that underneath there was somebody.
6	Check that the writing is formal and the vocabulary is precise and technical.	He had thrown it out of the window because he did not know that a person was underneath.

Now try these questions:

Achieved?

1 Rewrite these sentences formally.

a) Give us one of them sweets.

b) He should of been as sick as a parrot.

c) Me brother learned me to play the drums.

d) What did you do that for?

e) There isn't no pencils in the cupboard.

f) Can I have a lend of your stuff?

g) He should of had a fab day.

(2 marks each) /14

2 Rewrite this passage using Standard English.

> I were skiving with me mates on Monday afternoon, when I saw a well cool top. I so wanted it that I dunned one of me mates for the readies he lent from me. Don't know what he did that for. Anyways, I razzed the top and changed me mind 'cos I din't want it no more.

(10 marks) /10

3 Circle the correct word(s) to complete each sentence.

a) Louise did not eat (nothing / anything) at lunchtime.

b) The tiger could (of / have) deserted its cubs and escaped.

c) If necessary, pupils can (lend / borrow) items of equipment.

d) All the pupils were (learned / taught) how to cancel fractions.

e) The drink was (well / very) cool.

f) The elephant (does not / don't) like confined spaces.

g) The document will be ready (soon as / as soon as) possible.

(7 marks) /7

CHALLENGE Find a piece of formal writing and rewrite it informally.

Double negatives

Definition: The use of two negatives in a sentence is called a double negative.
The two negatives cancel each other out, so leaving a positive meaning.

Examples:

We didn't see nothing.
The two negatives in this sentence are didn't and nothing.
If we didn't see nothing that means we must have seen something.

I can't do no more.
The two negatives in this sentence are can't and no.
If I can't do no more that means I can do some more.

Let's practise!

What does the sentence actually mean?

Charlie couldn't walk no more.

1	Read the question, then read it again. What are you being asked to do?	**Write the sentence without the double negative, to show what the sentence really means.**
2	Find the negatives in the sentence.	**The negatives are couldn't and no.**
3	Work out how to get rid of the negatives.	**Could is the opposite of couldn't so we write: Charlie could walk no more. Some is the opposite of no so we write: Charlie could walk some more.**
4	Think about what the sentence means.	**If Charlie couldn't walk no more, that means Charlie could walk some more.**
5	Write the answer.	**Charlie could walk some more.**

TOP TIP

Double negatives used to be part of normal speech in English. Some parts of the country still use them every day in speech. However, they are not Standard English and should only be used in very informal writing. Learn to use a single negative instead!

TOP TIP

Answers

Page 7 Revision of word classes

Question 1 a) noun, verb **b)** adjective, adverb **c)** noun, verb, adjective **d)** noun, verb, adjective **e)** noun, verb

Question 2

Suddenly,	we	saw	a
ADV	PN	V	ART
shape	emerge	from	the
N	V	P	ART
shadows.			
N			

The	dogs	howled	because
ART	N	V	C
of	the	fireworks.	
P	ART	N	

Eat	healthy	foods	while
V	ADJ	N	C
you	are	growing.	
PN	V	V	

Although	it	is	cold,
C	PN	V	ADJ
I	am	going.	
PN	V	V	

Question 3 Answers will vary. Sample answers:

connective	article	adjective	noun
Consequently,	the	lazy	dog
verb	adverb		
grew	fatter.		

noun	verb	adverb	preposition
Mice	hide	quietly	under
article	noun	preposition	noun
the	sofa	at	home.

article	adjective	noun	verb
An	honest	man	pays
connective	pronoun	adverb	verb
while	you	unlawfully	steal.

Challenge Answers will vary. Sample answers:
Nouns: proper, common, countable, uncountable, mass, collective, concrete, abstract, pronouns

Verbs: auxiliary, lexical, dynamic, stative, finite, non-finite, regular, irregular, transitive, intransitive, causative

Adverb: place, time, manner, degree, quantity, frequency, affirmative, negation, interrogation, relative

Page 9 Nouns

Question 1

Abstract nouns	Collective nouns	Common nouns	Proper nouns	Uncountable nouns
art health weather electricity advice bravery curiosity fear happiness trust freedom	army company family audience	bag chair clarinet bus furniture	London Uncle Gary Harry New York English	art health weather electricity advice happiness trust (abstract nouns are usually uncountable)

Question 2 a) Charlotte's, anger, work, chocolate **b)** bunch, flowers, Miss Lomas's embarrassment **c)** Harvey, help, homework, Rio **d)** greed, children, problem, everyone **e)** school council, agreement, Mrs Hartley, playground equipment

Question 3 a) bevy **b)** herd / memory / parade **c)** colony / army / swarm **d)** gaggle **e)** litter **f)** pride **g)** lodge / colony **h)** parliament **i)** murder **j)** school / herd

Question 4 a) My first school was called Gleadless Primary School. **b)** The best book about cats is called The Cat Kingdom. **c)** My favourite uncle is Uncle Tom. **d)** At Headless Cross there is thought to be a headless ghost. **e)** Whaley Memorial Park is a fantastic park to visit.

Challenge Answers will vary. Sample answers: water, air, wood, cheese, snow, happiness, loneliness, freedom, fun, work, travel, sleep, information, understanding.

Page 11 Expanded noun phrases

Question 1

a) The old sensible lady

b) the tasty chocolate ice-cream.

c) a scented sticker.

d) my blue mountain bike.

e) an amazing comedy novel.

Question 2

the cake smelled delicious.	This is not an expanded noun phrase as 'sme led' is a verb.
my annoying little sister	This is an expanded noun phrase
the angry impatient teacher	This is an expanded noun phrase
his new sporty green bag was cool	Although there are adjectives, the verb 'was' is included so this is not an expanded noun phrase.
my heavy bag snapped	This is not an expanded noun phrase as the verb 'snapped' is used.

Question 3

Answers will vary, accept any appropriate expanded noun phrases ensuring there are no verbs. Sample answers:

Noun	Noun phrase
the table	the new glass table under the window
the book	the ancient torn book on the wooden shelf
the elephant	the young mischievous elephant from India

Page 13 Complex sentences

Question 1

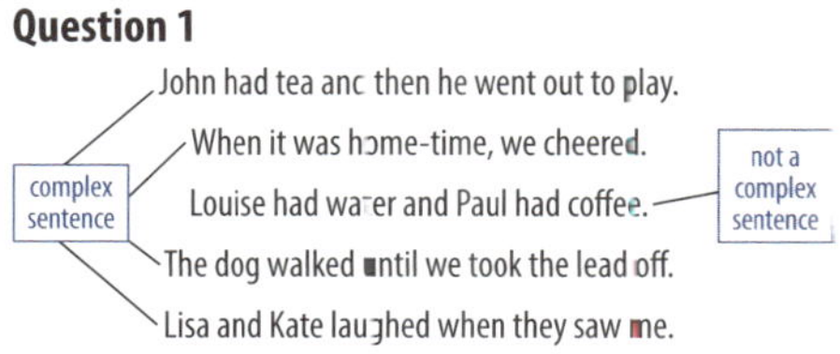

Question 2

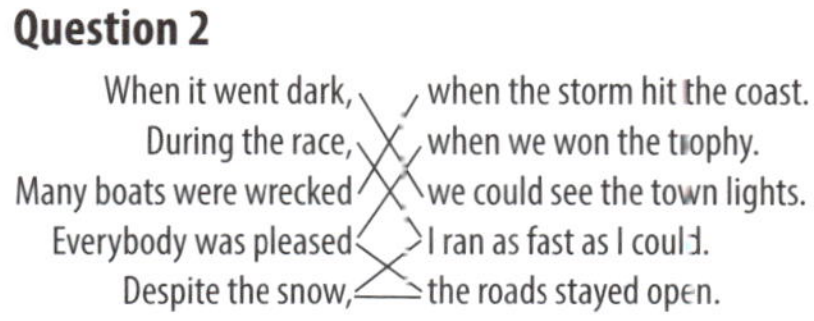

Question 3 a) we still had to put our coats on. **b)** We like to go out on our bikes **c)** we played with my new computer game. **d)** Never bring a phone to school **e)** Look after your pet

Question 4 a) Before I fall asleep, I like to read my book. **b)** My dad drives carefully when we are in the village. **c)** Even though I didn't sleep, I'm not really tired. **d)** Two children found the box when they were playing outside.

Question 5 Answers will vary. Sample answers: **a)** Before I went bowling **b)** whenever I could afford it **c)** As soon as he saw us

Challenge Answers will vary. Sample answers: The actor, during scene two, tripped over a prop then tore his costume whilst trying to get up.

Page 15 Phrases and clauses

Question 1 a) C **b)** C **c)** P **d)** C **e)** P **f)** C **g)** C **h)** C

Question 2 a) The dog whined when it heard the fireworks. **b)** Because it was snowing, we built a large snowman. **c)** We were allowed cake since it was my birthday. **d)** Reece fell down so we had to abandon the race. **e)** When Louie was away, we did a maths test.

Question 3

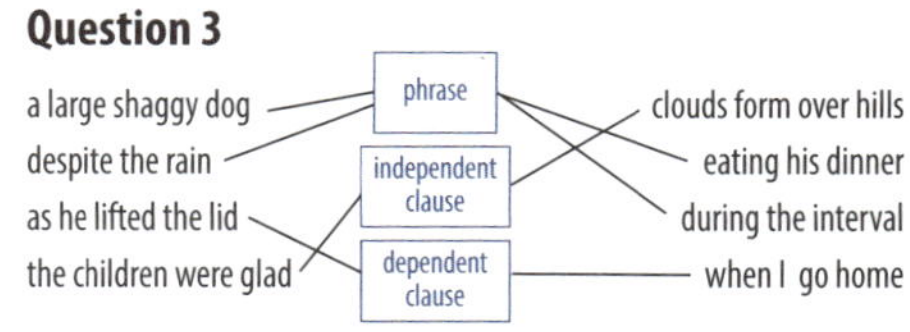

Question 4 a) Whilst watching the match, Sonal started to feel ill. **b)** The forest was dark and gloomy; the mountains were light and airy. **c)** The phone rang just as tea was ready. **d)** When he saw the bill, Sam was very cross.

Question 5 Answers will vary. Sample answers: **a)** While it was raining, we played indoors. **b)** Serena played on her computer after she finished her homework. **c)** I took my jumper off because it was hot.

Challenge Answers will vary. Which list is longest will depend on the type, complexity and style of text. Simple fiction will have more independent clauses because it uses less complex sentence structures. This is a chance for pupils to look at and evaluate a text while reflecting on the intended audience.

Page 17 Embedded clauses

Question 1 a) which was new **b)** which was too hot **c)** who wasn't holding the handlebars **d)** which was superb **e)** who was reading

Question 2 a) The art lesson, which lasted for one hour, involved modelling. **b)** Assemblies, which we have every day, are too long. **c)** Truck drivers, who often have to drive all day, have to take regular rest breaks. **d)** The farmer, who needed to harvest his hay, watched the weather forecast. **e)** Robert, who was frightened, ran into the house.

Question 3 a) No – the first comma is incorrectly placed. **b)** ✔ **c)** No – there is a sentence in the place of an embedded clause. **d)** No – the embedded clause is not complete. **e)** ✔

Question 4 Answers will vary. Check the embedded clauses and commas are correct. Sample answers: **a)** The house, which is down the road, is old. **b)** The car, which Dad has bought, is new. **c)** Children, who are funny, like telling jokes. **d)** Petrol, that makes some cars run, is very expensive. **e)** William, who enjoys electronic toys, likes using the robots.

Challenge Answers will vary. Pattern could be that plural nouns often work with and without commas.

Page 19 Active and passive sentences

Question 1

Andy was interested in sport.
The bus was hit by a car.
The man was arrested by the police.

active sentence
passive sentence

The class was taught by Mrs Butcher.
Caitlin won the race.
Vikki was tested by Mrs Sellars.

Question 2 a) P **b)** A **c)** P **d)** A

Question 3 a) The children had eaten the cake. **b)** The infants were spoiling the game. **c)** The audience appreciated the play. **d)** The snow is hiding the plants.

Question 4 a) Harvey is being chased by James. **b)** Skye is being laughed at by Megan. **c)** Ms Wright is being helped by Mrs Mellor.

Challenge Answers will vary. A comment could be that there are few passive voice sentences because they are harder to read and understand.

Page 21 Subject, object and verb

Question 1 a) The owl hoots. **b)** A lady screamed. **c)** The children were skipping. **d)** The bus stopped. **e)** They are busy. **f)** The fire-engine is red.

Question 2

Sentence	Subject	Object	Verb
The man washed the car.	man	car	washed
The trees were uprooted by the wind.	trees	wind	uprooted
Over the sea, the ship was sailing.	ship	sea	sailing
The traffic jam went through Manchester.	traffic jam	Manchester	went
Across the lawn danced the fairies.	fairies	lawn	danced

Question 3 a) object **b)** subject **c)** object **d)** subject **e)** subject

Question 4 Answers will vary. **a)** subject, sample answer: She **b)** verb, sample answer: missing **c)** subject, sample answer: they

Challenge Compound subjects = more than one subject. For example: Peter, Paul and Imran went out. Compound verbs = the subject does more than one thing. For example: I peeled the vegetables and sliced the meat. We laughed and sang all day.

Page 23 Adverbs and adverbials

Question 1 a) Jane sat with her legs crossed. **b)** The fan worked to cool the air. **c)** After the meal, Sam slept. **d)** When it rained, the children ran inside. **e)** Molly knocked because she wanted to come in.

Question 2 a) why? **b)** how long? **c)** how? **d)** where? **e)** when? **f)** how often?

Question 3 Answers will vary. Sample answers: **a)** The cat purred because she was content. **b)** The building collapsed last week. **c)** Lucy Mae practised the piano every day. **d)** Barti went to the park with his mates. **e)** Renata worked long and hard.

Question 4 Answers will vary. Sample answers: **a)** I am going to the park at the weekend. **b)** Sian is going for a walk by the canal. **c)** Make sure you take your medicine every three hours. **d)** Mum looked in to check how well we were doing. **e)** They are going on holiday for a fortnight.

Challenge Answers will vary. Connectives that might start adverbials include: so, before, after, because

Page 25 Connectives and cohesion

Questions 1 a) and 1 b)

Qualifying connectives although, however, unless, despite, except, if, as long as	**Illustrating connectives** such as, for example, for instance, as revealed by, in the case of
Contrasting connectives alternatively, whereas, instead of, otherwise, unlike,	**Adding connectives** also, moreover, and, as well as, too
Comparing connectives likewise, equally, in the same way, similarly, as with, like	**Cause and effect connectives** so, because, therefore, thus, consequently, since
Emphasising connectives in particular, especially, above all, significantly, indeed, notably	**Sequencing connectives** finally, next, then, first, meanwhile, eventually, after, before

Question 2

First part of the sentence	Connectives with conjunctions	Second part of the sentence
I peeled the vegetables	so, consequently,	Max lit the fire.
I was late	and, meanwhile,	someone answered the door.
I kept pressing the bell	until, eventually,	I missed the bus.
Everyone went on the trip	as well as	today was his birthday.
I did the shopping	especially as	cleaning the house.
I finished my work	except	lunchtime.
William was happy,	during	the boys who broke the window.

Challenge Answers will vary.

Page 27 Impersonal writing

Question 1 a) me, ecstatic **b)** we, (harmless, tortured) **c)** I, I **d)** you, me, (dangerous) **e)** we, I, (delighted)

Question 2

	Personal writing	Impersonal writing
I know that football teams have to travel a lot.	✔	
Pandas are at risk of extinction.		✔
Snakes are dangerous creatures that should be avoided.		✔
If I can do this, anybody can.	✔	
It is thought that children have to learn too much.		✔
Never make the same mistake that I did.	✔	
Dreadful, frightening events are threatening our survival.	✔	

Question 3

impersonal writing

Most countries have concerns.
Nobody would consider this idea.
Of course, Katy loves ice cream.
In my opinion, that would be a mistake.

personal writing

Question 4 Answers will vary. Sample answers: **a)** Cars go too fast. **b)** Some people think that spiders are brilliant. **c)** It can be thought that going sailing is enjoyable. **d)** Some people prefer red shirts. **e)** It was necessary to establish what was happening yesterday.

Challenge Answers will vary. Check that writing avoids personal pronouns and doesn't use emotive words to give away opinions.

Page 29 Formal writing and Standard English

Question 1 Answers will vary. Sample answers: **a)** Give me one of those sweets. **b)** He should have been ill. **c)** My brother taught me to play the drums. **d)** Why did you do that? **e)** There are no pencils in the cupboard. **f)** Can I borrow your equipment / belongings, please? **g)** He should have had a fabulous day.

Question 2 Answers will vary. Give 2 marks for verb–subject agreement, 2 marks for correct pronouns, 2 marks correctly structured sentences, 4 marks for slang corrected. Sample answer: I took a day away from school on Monday afternoon, when I saw an excellent top. I wanted the top, so demanded that a friend return the money he had borrowed from me for some unspecified purpose. I then looked closely at the top and decided against buying it.

Question 3 a) anything **b)** have **c)** borrow **d)** taught **e)** very **f)** does not **g)** as soon as

Challenge Answers will vary. Check that writing is formal and uses Standard English.

Page 31 Double negatives

Question 1 a), d), e) circled

Question 2 a) The boys will do that no more./ The boys won't do that any more. **b)** I broke nothing./ I didn't break anything. **c)** Nobody went anywhere./ Somebody went nowhere. **d)** Who will pay for no rides?/Who won't pay for any rides? **e)** Emanuela will not go./Emanuela won't go. **f)** He never heard anything./He heard nothing.

Question 3 a) The boys will do that some more / again. **b)** I did break something. **c)** Somebody went somewhere. **d)** Who will pay for some rides? **e)** Emanuela will go. **f)** He heard something

Question 4 a) A cake with one or more candles on it. **b)** An apple with one or more worms in it.

Question 5 When foxes hunt they don't have no mate to help them. They hunt less in summer because they don't have cubs to feed. Foxes can't hurt very large prey. They wouldn't have the strength to not run far.

Challenge Answers will vary. Often an odd number of negatives has a negative meaning, and an even number of negatives has a positive meaning.

Page 33 Modal verbs

Question 1 a) should **b)** might **c)** would **d)** will **e)** must

Question 2 Answers will vary. Sample answers:

Example	Explanation
Nadien should ride his bike.	This means that Nadien has less of a choice, should suggests there is a strong reason that he should ride his bike.
Nadien would ride his bike.	This means that Nadien usually does this.
Nadien might ride his bike.	This means that Nadien has an option to ride his bike and that the choice is his.

Question 3 Answers will vary. Sample answers – must be punctuated accurately:
Could – I could spend all of my money on that watch if I wanted to.
Might – I might go to America this year for my holidays.
Should – Mum should wash the car whilst the weather is good.
Must – I must buy a new washing machine, the old one has broken.

Can – Ashley can complete the obstacle course in less than two minutes now.

Question 4

Positive form	Negative form
should	shouldn't
could	couldn't
can	can't
must	mustn't
would	wouldn't

Page 35 Commas

Question 1 a) ✔ **b)** N **c)** N **d)** N **e)** ✔

Question 2 a) E, E **b)** E, E, L, J

Question 3 a) Andy, trying to be helpful, piled up the boots, coats and hats. **b)** Whilst reading a story, I noticed the window was open. **c)** "You can do that, can't you?" asked Lisa. **d)** ✔ **e)** I do well in maths, reading and science, but I do best in writing.

Question 4 a) Annie received money, books and toys for her birthday, which was yesterday. **b)** Alli pleaded, "Please, James, you will play, won't you?"

Challenge Answers will vary. Check that commas have been used correctly.

Page 37 Speech

Question 1 a) "Watch this," whispered Mark. "He's going to open the cupboard door." **b)** "If," intoned Mr Pattison, "I hear anyone say, 'It's not fair,' I will be very upset." **c)** "Stop!" called the policeman, "or I will arrest you." (Or may have a capital letter.) **d)** "He is," stated Kerry, "a very silly boy."

Question 2 a) "Don't worry," said Pat, "we'll find it." **b)** "Perhaps," mused Andy, "You could make more of an effort." **c)** "Tom said, 'I'm coming,' but I told him he couldn't," confessed Barti. **d)** "If Lani said that Rob said that you said 'I don't want to go,' then I believe her," said Ruby.

Question 3 Give 2 marks for correctly placed speech marks, 2 marks for starting a new line for each new speaker, 2 marks for punctuation within speech marks (capital or not and punctuation before second " for each pair).

"When the weather is sunny," said Max, "it's good to go out."

"It's good to go out anyway!" retorted Rowan.

"Yes," agreed Isidore, "because my mum said, 'If you stay in the house any longer I think I'll go mad,' and she did look like she was losing it."

"Yes," said Rowan, "and I think my mum has the same problem!"

Question 4

	Is it correct?	If not, explain why not.
"Sit up," said the teacher, "And look this way."		A capital letter on 'And', which is the middle of the speech sentence.
"Mum said, 'No, you can't!'" said Eleanor.		Double inverted commas used for the quote.
"Let's rest," suggested George, "before we walk any further."	✔	
"Well, she was surprised. 'Never mind' I told her – you can't win them all!" laughed Nan.		Needs a comma after 'mind'.
"Rest," ordered John, "before you do any more work."	✔	
"Two weeks," I informed him, 'So don't say, 'No-one told me,' because I'm telling you now."		A capital letter on 'So' which is the middle of the speech sentence.

Challenge Answers will vary. Sample answer:
"She ordered us to 'Watch and learn!' so we did," laughed Tom.
"What happened?" asked Lucy curiously.
"Well," he replied, "she jumped on one side of the boat and fell straight off the other!"

Page 39 Hyphens

Question 1 a) accident-prone **b)** computer-aided **c)** good-looking **d)** sugar-free **e)** power-driven

Question 2

custom-built	built to the customer's specification
ex-husband	man that someone used to be married to
camera-ready	ready to be filmed
self-pity	feeling sorry for yourself
mayor-elect	the person selected to be the next mayor
all-inclusive	everything paid for

Question 3 Answers will vary. Sample answers:
a) The quick-thinking girl managed to put out the fire. **b)** The bad-tempered boy wasn't very popular. **c)** The muddle-headed professor mixed up the experiment. **d)** The co-owner of the gym was a fitness instructor. **e)** Seventy-six balloons went up into the sky.

Question 4 a) fifty-five **b)** seventy-one **c)** two-thirds **d)** ninety-eight **e)** twenty-seven **f)** forty-three

Challenge Answers will vary. Sample answers: put-upon – taken advantage of; snarl-up – traffic jam or muddle.

Page 41 Ellipses

Question 1

	Words missed out	A speaker trailed off	To show a pause
The fireman said, "… it was started deliberately."	✔		
"I'm not sure …" whispered Caitlin.		✔	
Ofsted reported that the children … behaved well.	✔		
Rowan waited … and waited … and waited.			✔
"Please … stop it … don't …" shouted Charlotte.			✔
"I wonder …" said Mrs Butcher.		✔	

Question 2 a) to show words have been missed out **b)** to show pauses in speech **c)** to show a speaker trailed off **d)** to show words missed out **e)** to show a pause in the action

Question 3 Answers may vary. Award 2 marks if all unnecessary information is removed and 1 mark for a good attempt. **a)** The house … could be dangerous … so it has to be demolished. **b)** If you go swimming in a lake … wear a wet suit … and always have someone … with you.

Challenge Answers will vary. Pupils may find that fiction books use ellipses more for speakers trailing off or to show pauses, while non-fiction books use ellipses more to show that words have been missed out (for example, from quotes).

Page 43 Parentheses

Question 1

	Explain a word	Emphasise a point	Show what the writer is thinking	Add extra information
(though I don't think that is true)			✔	
– in other words, your skull –	✔			
, who was tall and thin,				✔
– and I mean really tall.		✔		
(a set of lines for writing music)	✔			
– what a stupid idea.			✔	
(its babies live in there for six weeks)				✔

Question 2 b), c) and **e)** ticked

Question 3 Answers may vary. Sample answers: **a)** Tim always got his own way. He was spoilt. **b)** The paediatrician visited the ward. She is the children's doctor. **c)** The teacher was being unfair about the party. I thought he was really unfair.
d) Some people do what I ask straight away. They are usually the intelligent ones.

Question 4 a) The Owls (who are based in Hillsborough, Sheffield) are a great football team. **b)** Tigers (with their excellent camouflage) are magnificent hunters. **c)** My favourite day (apart from my birthday) is the end of term. **d)** Algebra (maths with letters) is lots of fun.

Challenge Answers will vary. Sample answer:
The party, which was in the village square, was enjoyed by everyone (even Mrs Pims – probably, anyway). Gill – she's my best friend now – baked a cake. She called it a roulade (a cake made with meringue and cream) which was delicious – really delicious!

Page 45 Prefixes

Question 1 international, transnational, mid-Atlantic, transatlantic, semiconscious, hyperconscious, interactive, hyperactive

Question 2 a) script; date; mortem; natal **b)** gone hand; thought; name **c)** lace; view; weave; marry **d)** rational; resolute; replaceable; religious

Question 3 Answers may vary. Sample answers:
a) transaction, transport, transform, transplant **b)** irregular, irrespective, irreproachable, irreversible, irreverent **c)** mid-air, midwinter, midsummer, midway, mid-week, midship
d) interbreed, interchange, intergalactic, interplanetary, intercourse, interweave **e)** anti-aircraft, anti-personnel, anticlockwise, antidote, anticlimax

Question 4 a) transformed **b)** irresistible

Question 5 Answers will vary. Sample answers: **a)** prevent freezing **b)** before midday
c) a larger than normal supermarket **d)** half joined
e) the land in the middle **f)** not responsible
g) somebody that stars with someone else **h)** after the war

Challenge Answers will vary. Sample answers:

ante–	before	anteroom, antecedent
counter–	opposite, opposition	counteract, counter-attack, counter-clockwise
under–	below	underarm, undercarriage, undersecretary, underwear
aut(o)–	self	automatic, autobiography, autopilot
mal–	bad(ly)	malnutrition, malpractice
mon(o)–	one, single	monorail, monocle, monotony

Page 47 Suffixes

Question 1 a) satisfy **b)** art **c)** gang **d)** friend **e)** adventure **f)** god

Question 2 a) child, new, fool, sweet **b)** collect, decorate, rotate, direct **c)** dental, piano, chemistry, science **d)** great, sick, sweet, thick

Question 3 Answers will vary. Sample answers: **a)** collision, decision, revision **b)** conscious, delicious, ridiculous **c)** advertise, harmonise, trivialise **d)** demonic, realistic, characteristic **e)** murderess, stewardess, waitress

Question 4 a) realistic **b)** privacy **c)** collision

Question 5 Answers will vary. Sample answers: **a)** a person who plays the cello **b)** something that has style **c)** in the state of rotating **d)** in the process of being forgiven **e)** show on / make for television **f)** a female prince / daughter of a king and queen

Challenge Answers will vary. Check that pupils have found the correct meaning for each suffix.

Page 49 Plurals

Question 1 a) ditches **b)** hoaxes **c)** lorries **d)** leaves **e)** counters **f)** pianos **g)** gases **h)** potatoes

Question 2 a) men **b)** feet **c)** people **d)** appendices (accept appendixes) **e)** mice **f)** these **g)** oxen **h)** fungi (allow funguses)

Question 3 moose, spaghetti, headquarters, tuna, bison

Question 4 Answers will vary. Sample answers: **a)** We stopped at the crossroads. All the crossroads were blocked off. **b)** The sheep was big. The sheep were frightened. **c)** The piece of furniture was delivered. We put the bedroom furniture into the hall.

d) Westies are a species of dog. Every species is part of a classification group.

Challenge Answers will vary. Sample answers: deer / deer; moose / moose; salmon / salmon; stigma / stigmatai; louse /lice; goose / geese.

Page 51 Homophones and similar words

Question 1 Answers will vary but check that these meanings are conveyed: **a)** affect (verb), to affect the outcome; effect (noun) the result or outcome or (verb) to effect so that it makes or brings about **b)** aloud, out loud; allowed, permitted **c)** farther, a distance away; father, a male parent **d)** altar, a religious table; alter, change **e)** compliment, to make nice remarks; complement, to make something complete or better **f)** profit, money gained; prophet, someone who foretells the future **g)** whose, possessive pronoun (shows something belongs to someone); who's, contraction of 'who is' or 'who has' **h)** advice, (noun) a piece of advice; advise, to recommend what someone should do **i)** past (noun / adjective) referring to time or (preposition / adverb) showing direction or place; passed, past tense of 'to pass' **j)** cereal, made from grain; serial, things that happen one after the other **k)** principal, the most important or the person in charge; principle, a truth or belief.

Challenge Answers will vary. Sample answers: knight (a medieval soldier) / night (after the sun has gone down); mail (what is received in the post) / male (a man); flea (an insect) / flee (run away); meat (food from an animal) / meet (get together); medal (a prize for winning) / meddle (interfere); sweet (pudding)/ suite (set of).

Page 53 Synonyms and antonyms

Question 1 a) terminate **b)** commission **c)** determined **d)** abundance **e)** atrocious

Question 2 a) confident, wary **b)** envious, content **c)** failure, triumph

Question 3 a) buy, sell **b)** entrance, exit

Question 4 Sentence answers will vary. The correct antonyms are: **a)** export / import **b)** departure / arrival **c)** overweight / underweight **d)** interior / exterior **e)** victory / defeat **f)** insult / compliment

Challenge Answers will vary. Sample answer: suffocation / asphyxiation.

Page 55 Figurative language

Question 1

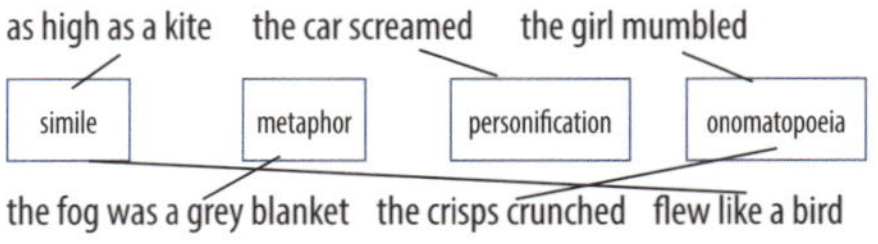

Question 2 Answers will vary. Standard similes are given here: **a)** a giraffe **b)** a ghost / sheet **c)** an owl / Solomon **d)** a bear / wolf **e)** a lion **f)** a peacock **g)** a post **h)** a bat **i)** a bee **j)** an eel

Question 3 a) tick tock **b)** smash **c)** buzz **d)** click **e)** sizzle **f)** quack

Question 4 Answers will vary. Sample answers:

The bus	was as slow as a snail.
	was a people-eating monster.
	grumbled all the way up the hill.
	crashed.
The flowers	were as white as snow.
	were stars scattered on the grass.
	waved as we walked past.
	whispered.
The wind	was as fierce as a tiger.
	was a roaring, fighting beast.
	whistled happily as it danced around the chimney.
	whooshed.

Challenge Answers will vary, but should refer to the picture or effect the author was trying to create. (Do not accept general answers such as 'for emphasis' or 'to show what it was like'.)

Page 57 Idioms

Question 1 Answers will vary. Sample answers: **a)** lend a hand – help out **b)** raining cats and dogs – raining heavily **c)** jump to it – hurry up **d)** cost an arm and a leg – very expensive **e)** racing against the clock – hurrying

Question 2 Answers will vary. Sample answers: **a)** Given as an example. **b)** She was wearing designer clothes that were right over the top! **c)** He was making such a noise I told him to pipe down. **d)** Tongue in cheek, he said, "Let's go skating at midnight." **e)** After breaking the picture, Jerry broke the lamp, which was the last straw.

Question 3 Blood is thicker than water.

Challenge Answers will vary. Sample answers: up and running; beat about the bush; catch one's eye; couch potato; get on one's nerves; in over one's head; in the red; pull someone's leg; sleep on it; wet behind the ears.

Page 59 Etymology

Word		Etymology
alarm		Chinese – *ke-tsiap* was a sauce invented at the end of the 17th century.
ketchup		Italian – means 'To arms!'
robot		French – means good air. In the Middle Ages if you smelled good you were thought to be healthier and happier.
bungalow		Old German – *hus* means 'house' and *bunda* means 'owner'. A homeowner would be a good person to marry!
debonair		Hindi – means 'one-storey house'.
husband		Latin – *liber* means 'to peel' and would refer to the inner bark of a tree that manuscripts were written on.
library		Italian – small ball or pebble that was used to cast a vote in a box.
ballot		Czech – means 'worker'.
salary		Latin – Roman soldiers were paid a handful of salt a day, which was replaced by money as it was easier to transport, so soldiers' got their salt money (*salarium*).
sinister		Old English – *stol* for 'throne'.
stool		Old French – means 'cooked twice'.
biscuit		Latin for 'left'; the left side was thought to be evil.

Question 1

Examples
aquamarine, aquarium, aqueduct, aquifer, aquadrome
automobile, autonomy, autograph, automatic
globe, global, globule, globular
microscope, microphone, micro-organism

Question 2 Answers will vary. Sample answers:

Meaning
alone
death
life

Question 3

Challenge Answers will vary. Sample answers: Latin, Greek, Spanish, Italian, French, German.

Now try these questions:

Achieved? ☺ 😐 ☹

1 Circle the sentences that have double negatives.

a) Don't eat no more.
b) You can't play there.
c) The birds don't sing so well in the city.
d) A girl can't buy no flowers.
e) The chair isn't uncomfortable.

(1 mark each) /5

2 Write these sentences with only one negative.

a) The boys won't do that no more. ____________
b) I didn't break nothing. ____________
c) Nobody went nowhere. ____________
d) Who won't pay for no rides? ____________
e) Emanuela won't not go. ____________
f) He never heard nothing. ____________

(1 mark for each line) /6

3 Write what these sentences actually mean.

a) The boys won't do that no more. ____________
b) I didn't break nothing. ____________
c) Nobody went nowhere. ____________
d) Who won't pay for no rides? ____________
e) Emanuela won't not go. ____________
f) He never heard nothing. ____________

(1 mark for each line) /6

4 Complete the pictures to show the meaning of each sentence.

The cake didn't have no candles.

The apple hadn't got no worms in it.

(1 mark each) /2

5 Underline the sentences that have double negatives.

When foxes hunt they don't have no mate to help them. They hunt less in summer because they don't have cubs to feed. Foxes can't hunt very large prey. They wouldn't have the strength to not run far.

(1 mark each) /2

CHALLENGE How many negatives can you write in one sentence? Work out whether your sentence has a positive or a negative meaning.

Modal verbs

Definition: Modal verbs are also called auxiliary verbs and are used to help the main verb.

Modal verbs are;

- can / could
- will / would
- shall / should
- may / might
- must / ought

For example:

I might go shopping later. You should carry the bags for Gran.

Let's practise!

Add a modal verb to complete the sentence.

John wondered if he ____________ complete his homework before or after his dinner.

1	Read the question, then read it again. What are you being asked to do?	**Add a modal verb to complete the sentence.**
2	Remind yourself what modal verbs are.	**They are verbs that help the main verb.**
3	Identify the main verb in the sentence.	**The main verb is complete.**
4	Say some modal verbs aloud.	**Can, could, will, would, shall, should, may, might, must, ought.**
5	Choose a modal verb to insert.	**could**
6	Check if it makes sense.	**John wondered if he COULD complete his homework before or after his dinner.**
7	Try alternative modals and decide which one best completes the sentence.	**Possible answers: can, could, will, would, shall should, may, might, must**

TOP TIP

Modal verbs have positive and negative forms.
When writing a modal in its negative form, you must use the apostrophe accurately. For example:
'You **shouldn't** run in the corridors.'

TOP TIP

Now try these questions:

Achieved? ☺ 😐 ☹

1 Circle the modal verb in each sentence.

a) The concert should finish at 10 p.m.
b) I might be able to fix your radiator for you.
c) Dermot knew he would be late for his meeting.
d) I will meet you tomorrow night if you like?
e) Jackie told Freddie he must eat all of his rice.

(1 mark each) /5

2 How does changing the modal verb change the meaning of the sentence? Explain your answer. One has been done for you.

Example	Explanation
Nadien could ride his bike.	*This means that Nadien has an option to ride his bike and that the choice to do so is his.*
Nadien should ride his bike.	
Nadien would ride his bike.	
Nadien might ride his bike.	

(1 mark each) /3

3 Make up a sentence using each of these modal verbs.

could ______________________________

might ______________________________

should ______________________________

must ______________________________

can ______________________________

(1 mark each) /5

4 Complete the table to show the positive and negative forms of modal verbs.

Positive form	Negative form
should	shouldn't
	couldn't
can	
	mustn't
would	

(1 mark each) /4

Commas

You should already know how to use commas in these ways:

- to separate speech from the speaker (if no other punctuation is used)
- to separate items in a list (replacing the word and or or)
- after extra information is added at the start of a sentence (a fronted adverbial).

Other uses of the comma include:

- before the words and, or, but, yet or while when they join two sentences:
  The rehearsal is tomorrow, but I have my induction day at high school then.
- to separate extra information in a sentence (usually used in pairs):
  Matthew, during playtime, banged his head.
- to separate the name or title of a person being directly addressed:
  "Will you, Abnir, go and fetch the technology trolley?"
- to separate a question from a statement: You will come, won't you?

Let's practise!

Put commas where they are needed in this sentence.

Jaquin took the long difficult path which was very steep all the way to the top but I didn't.

Step	What to do	Answer
1	Read the question, then read it again. What are you being asked to do?	Put the commas into the sentence.
2	Check if there is any speech.	No.
3	Check if there is a list.	Long difficult path. Could they be separated by and? Yes – long and difficult path – so put a comma between them.
4	Check if there is extra information added.	Which was very steep could be removed from the sentence, so put commas before and after it.
5	Check for the words and, or, but, yet and while then check if there are complete sentences before and after them.	Yes – the word but is used and there is a complete sentence before and after it, so use a comma before it.
6	Is there a question and a statement? Or is someone being directly addressed?	No.
7	Write your answer with the commas.	Jaquin took the long, difficult path, which was very steep, all the way to the top, but I didn't.

Now try these questions:

Achieved? ☺ 😐 ☹

1 Tick the sentences where the commas are used correctly.

a) Imogen, Vanessa and Jonathan, who live in Wales, keep hens.
b) She wanted to do her homework, as well as go to the park, to play.
c) When I laugh, it makes me sneeze, if I have hay fever.
d) Only yesterday, Olivia was making a theatre when, unfortunately it broke.
e) After tea, we watched a video, which was extremely funny, until it was time to leave.

(1 mark for each line) /5

2 In each box, write an **E** if the comma separates extra information from the sentence; an **L** if it is used in a list; or a **J** if it is used before **and**, **or**, **but**, **yet** or **while** to join two sentences.

a) The monster, which breathed poisonous gas, turned to me.

b) The shop, which was tiny, sold papers, drinks and snacks, and we bought the lot!

(1 mark each) /6

3 Check the commas in these sentences. Tick them if they are correct and rewrite them correctly if they are not.

a) Andy, trying to be helpful, piled up the boots coats and hats.

____

b) Whilst reading a story I noticed the window, was open.

____

c) "You can do that can't you?," asked Lisa.

____

d) The eagle, soaring overhead, scanned the area, hunting prey.

____

e) I do well in maths, reading, and science but I do best in writing.

____

(1 mark for each line) /5

4 Put commas where they are needed in these sentences.

a) Annie received money books and toys for her birthday which was yesterday.
b) Alli pleaded "Please James you will play won't you?"

(1 mark for each line) /2

CHALLENGE

Write the title The Journey on a piece of paper or in your book. Write sentences linked to the title, using commas in all the ways shown in this section. Your writing can be factual or fictional.

Speech

By Level 5 you need to be expert at punctuating speech. Let's review the basic rules.

Rules for punctuating speech:

- Put " " around what the speaker says.
- A new speech sentence starts with a capital letter (even if it is in the middle of another sentence).
- Separate what was said from the speaker with a comma unless there is already a ? or an !
- Start a new paragraph if a new speaker says something.

At Level 5 you should also be able to apply these speech rules:

- When quoting another speaker in direct speech, use single inverted commas: "I asked where she was going but she said, 'Mind your own business'," I told them.
- Only put a capital letter after the first speech marks if it's the start of a speech sentence: "Well," complained Georgia, "she didn't have to say it like that." Notice that the she at the start of the second speech marks does not have a capital letter because it is not the start of the speech sentence.

Let's practise!

Punctuate the speech in this sentence correctly.

anyway said Evie why did she shout go away like that?

Step	What to do	Answer
1	Read the question, then read it again. What are you being asked to do?	Punctuate the speech in the sentence.
2	Work out exactly what was said and put " " around the words.	Evie said: anyway why did she shout go away like that? So we write: "anyway" said Evie "why did she shout go away like that?"
3	Start the speech sentence with a capital letter and separate the speech from the speaker with commas.	"Anyway," said Evie, "why did she shout go away like that?"
4	Check if there is a quotation in the speech.	Yes – someone shouted "go away".
5	Put single inverted commas around the quote, start the speech sentence with a capital letter and use commas to separate the quote from the rest of the sentence.	"Anyway," said Evie, "why did she shout, 'Go away,' like that?" If 'Go away,' was shouted it needs to end with an exclamation mark. "Anyway," said Evie, "why did she shout, 'Go away!' like that?"

Now try these questions:

Achieved? ☺ 😐 ☹

1 Put the capital letters and speech punctuation in the correct places in these sentences.

a) watch this whispered mark. he's going to open the cupboard door.
b) if intoned mr pattison i hear anyone say, it's not fair, i will be very upset.
c) stop called the policeman or i will arrest you.
d) he is stated kerry a very silly boy.

(1 mark for each line) /4

2 Circle the errors in this speech punctuation.

a) "Don't worry said Pat, we'll find it."
b) "Perhaps," mused Andy, You could make more of an effort."
c) "Tom said, "I'm coming," but I told him he couldn't", confessed Barti.
d) "If Lani said that Rob said that you said I don't want to go, then I believe her," said Ruby.

(1 mark for each line) /4

3 Rewrite this paragraph, punctuating it correctly.

When the weather is sunny said Max its good to go out. It's good to go out anyway retorted Rowan. Yes agreed Isidore because my mum said if you stay in the house any longer I think I'll go mad and she did look like she was losing it. Yes said Rowan and I think my mum has the same problem.

____

____

____

____

(6 marks) /6

4 Tick the sentences that are correctly punctuated.

	Is it correct?	If not, explain why not.
"Sit up," said the teacher, "And look this way."		
"Mum said, "No, you can't!"" said Eleanor.		
"Let's rest," suggested George, "before we walk any further."		
"Well, she was surprised. 'Never mind' I told her – you can't win them all!" laughed Nan.		
"Rest," ordered John, "before you do any more work."		
"Two weeks," I informed him, "So don't say, 'No one told me,' because I'm telling you now."		

(1 mark for each row) /6

CHALLENGE Write a dialogue that illustrates all the rules of speech.

Hyphens

Definition: Hyphens are short dashes between two words.
For example, forget-me-not.

Hyphens are used for	Examples
some compound nouns	mother-in-law, hang-glider
verbs made from two nouns	to ice-skate, to court-martial
compound adjectives	green-fingered, long-eared
adding a prefix to some words	ex-wife, re-examine
clarity, to distinguish words	re-sign / resign, re-creation / recreation
writing fractions and numbers less than 100 as words	one-sixth, forty-six

Let's practise!

Match these compound words with their meanings.

green-fingered	not being open to new ideas
long-eared	easy-going
happy-go-lucky	smart
well-dressed	good at growing things
narrow-minded	having long ears

1. Read the question, then read it again. What are you being asked to do?

Match the words to their meanings.

2. Look for any words that you are confident you know.

Long-eared must mean having long ears. Well-dressed must mean smart.

3. Check the words and meanings that are left.

green-fingered	**not being open to new ideas**
happy-go-lucky	**easy-going**
narrow-minded	**good at growing things**

4. Select the most appropriate meanings.

Green-fingered sounds like it is to do with growing things. Happy-go-lucky sounds like easy-going, which leaves narrow-minded as not being open to new ideas.

5. Join the words to their meanings.

green-fingered	**not being open to new ideas**
long-eared	**easy-going**
happy-go-lucky	**smart**
well-dressed	**good at growing things**
narrow-minded	**having long ears**

Now try these questions:

Achieved? ☺ 😐 ☹

1 Underline the compound adjectives in these sentences.

a) Joe has always been accident-prone.
b) The computer-aided research was very expensive.
c) Mr Kwec was a good-looking man.
d) The juice was supposed to be sugar-free.
e) The power-driven teacher wanted to be a head teacher.

(1 mark each) /5

2 Match each compound word to its meaning.

custom-built	ready to be filmed
ex-husband	man that someone used to be married to
camera-ready	built to the customer's specification
self-pity	feeling sorry for yourself
mayor-elect	everything paid for
all-inclusive	the person selected to be the next mayor

(1 mark each) /6

3 Write a sentence for each of these compound words.

a) quick-thinking ______________________________

____

b) bad-tempered ______________________________

____

c) muddle-headed ______________________________

____

d) co-owner ______________________________

____

e) seventy-six ______________________________

____

(1 mark each) /5

4 Write these numbers correctly as words

a) 55 ______________ **b)** 71 ______________
c) $^2/_3$ ______________ **d)** 98 ______________
e) 27 ______________ **f)** 43 ______________

(1 mark each) /6

CHALLENGE

Find some hyphenated words in a reading book.
Write them down and explain what they mean.

Ellipses

Definition: An ellipsis is a set of three dots …

Use ellipses in formal writing when a word or words are missed out of a quote:

The mayor said, "Our schools give the best education …"

Use ellipses in informal writing to show characters trailing off in speech:

"Perhaps they won't mind …" stammered Alex.

or to show pauses for emphasis or thought:

She looked … she waited … she crossed.

Let's practise!

Use an ellipsis to shorten this quote so that just the main message is written.

The head teacher, in assembly, said, "After careful thought, having considered the problem from every angle, I have come to a decision. Because there are too many children to fit into the hall, I have decided that there will be two sittings at lunchtime, with the younger children eating first, and then the older children going in after that. I hope you all understand why that is necessary."

1. Read the question, then read it again. What are you being asked to do?

   Give the important message from the quote.

2. Underline the important information.

   The head teacher, in assembly, said, "After careful thought, having considered the problem from every angle, I have come to a decision. Because there are too many children to fit into the hall, I have decided that there will be two sittings at lunchtime, with the younger children eating first, and then the older children going in after that. I hope you all understand why that is necessary."

3. Write the important information, putting an ellipsis where words have been missed out.

   The head-teacher … said, "I have come to a decision … I have decided that there will be two sittings at lunchtime …"

TOP TIP Don't overuse the ellipsis. It loses its impact if there are too many in your writing. **TOP TIP**

Now try these questions:

Achieved? ☺ 😐 ☹

1 Complete the table to show why an ellipsis has been used.

	Words missed out	A speaker trailed off	To show a pause
The fireman said, " … it was started deliberately."			
"I'm not sure …" whispered Caitlin.			
Ofsted reported that the children … behaved well.			
Rowan waited … and waited … and waited.			
"Please … stop it … don't …" shouted Charlotte.			
"I wonder …" said Mrs Butcher.			

(1 mark each) /6

2 Explain why an ellipsis has been used in each sentence.

a) The police report stated that the man … was dangerous.

____

b) "Steer to the left … no, to the right … no, to the left!" called Callum.

____

c) "If you did that …" said Ms Moore, thoughtfully.

____

d) In court the verdict … was guilty.

____

e) They saw the fox … the fox saw them.

____

(1 mark each) /5

3 Write the important messages from these quotes, using an ellipsis to show where words have been missed out.

a) The house, which has been left empty for years and years, is falling apart. It could be dangerous if people try to go inside so it has to be demolished.

____

b) If you go swimming in a lake, which can be very dangerous, especially if the water is cold, you need to take precautions: wear a wet suit, which is suitable for swimming activities, and always have someone on the bank or with you in the water in case you get into difficulties.

____

(2 marks for each line) /4

CHALLENGE

Look through books in the library and write down any uses of the ellipsis you find. Keep a note of books where a lot of ellipses are used. What type of books are they?

Parentheses

Definition: A parenthesis is an extra word or phrase that is put into a sentence. It can be used to:

- show what someone is thinking
- add extra information for the reader
- explain the meaning of a word
- emphasise a point.

Parentheses are usually written in brackets, between commas or between dashes.

Examples:

a) Adam (who is rather strange) collects plastic bottles.
b) Adam – who is rather strange – collects plastic bottles.
c) Adam, who is rather strange, collects plastic bottles.

Let's practise!

Remove the brackets from this sentence and write the same information in two sentences.

The Statue of Liberty (standing in the harbour at New York) was a symbol of hope to all immigrants to America.

Step		
1	Read the question, then read it again. What are you being asked to do?	**Remove the brackets and put information into two sentences.**
2	Write the sentence given without the information in brackets (the parenthesis).	**The Statue of Liberty was a symbol of hope to all immigrants to America.**
3	Read the information that was in brackets.	**(standing in the harbour at New York)**
4	Make it into a complete sentence.	**The Statue of Liberty stands in the harbour in New York.**
5	Read the sentences together – do you need to change any words?	**The Statue of Liberty is used in both sentences so we could replace it in one with a pronoun.**
6	Decide on an order for the sentences and write your final answer.	**The Statue of Liberty stands in the harbour in New York. It was a symbol of hope to all immigrants to America.**

TOP TIP

- If your sentence contains hyphens, avoid using dashes as they look very similar. Use brackets or commas instead.
- If your sentence already contains commas, avoid using commas as it will get rather confusing to read! Use brackets or dashes instead.

TOP TIP

Now try these questions:

Achieved? ☺ 😐 ☹

1 Complete the table to show the function of the parentheses:

	Explain a word	Emphasise a point	Show what the writer is thinking	Add extra information
(though I don't think that is true)				
– in other words, your skull –				
, who was tall and thin,				
– and I mean really tall.				
(a set of lines for writing music)				
– what a stupid idea.				
(its babies live in there for six weeks)				

(1 mark each) /7

2 Tick the sentences where the parenthesis is correctly used.

a) Jack and Kerry always (went to) town.
b) The fermata (or pause sign) is frequently used in music.
c) My dad is fantastic at cooking (or so he thinks).
d) The car which was new (had cost a lot of money).
e) Imran (being a natural at art) always got to help with the stage backdrop.

(1 mark for each line) /5

3 Remove the brackets from these sentences and write the same information in two sentences each time.

a) Tim (who was spoilt) always got his own way.

____

b) The paediatrician (children's doctor) visited the ward.

____

c) The teacher was being unfair (and I mean really unfair) about the party.

____

d) Some people (usually the intelligent ones) do what I ask straight away.

____

(1 mark for each line) /4

4 Add the missing brackets in these sentences.

a) The Owls who are based in Hillsborough, Sheffield are a great football team.
b) Tigers with their excellent camouflage are magnificent hunters.
c) My favourite day apart from my birthday is the end of term.
d) Algebra maths with letters is lots of fun.

(1 mark each) /4

CHALLENGE Write a description of a party using different types of parenthesis in your writing.

Prefixes

Definition: A prefix is a group of letters placed at the start of a word.
The prefix changes the meaning of the word.
Knowing prefixes can make spelling easier and increase your vocabulary.

Examples: Some common prefixes with their meanings are:

Prefix	Meaning	Examples
anti– ant–	against / opposite to	antibiotic, Antarctic,
fore–	before	forefinger, foreshadow
inter–	between	interact, interface
post–	after	postpone, postnatal
co–	together	co-education, coordinate
il–	not	illegal, illiberal
ir–	not	irrelevant, irredeemable
mid–	in the middle of	midterm, midnight
semi–	half	semi-conscious, semicircle
hyper–	more than normal	hypersonic, hyperbole
trans–	across	translate, transnational

Let's practise!

Use your knowledge of prefixes to write the meaning of these words.

hypercritical **semi-precious**

Step		
1	Read the question, then read it again. What are you being asked to do?	**Work out the meaning of the words.**
2	Look at the first word and think what the prefix means.	hypercritical – hyper– **means more than normal.**
3	Use this to give the meaning of the word.	hypercritical **means more critical than is normal.**
4	Look at the second word and think what the prefix means.	semi-precious – semi– **means half.**
5	Use this to give the meaning of the word.	semi-precious **means half precious, so that is valuable but not really expensive.**

Now try these questions:

Achieved? ☺ 😐 ☹

1 Use prefixes from the table on the previous page with each of these words to make two different words.

_______ national _______ Atlantic _______ conscious _______ active
_______ national _______ Atlantic _______ conscious _______ active

(1 mark each) /8

2 Circle the four words on each line that would go with these prefixes.

a) post– script date mortem reason natal figure
b) fore– ward gone hundred hand thought list name
c) inter– lace sense stop view weave live marry
d) ir– rational racial resolute reduce replaceable religious react

(1 mark each) /16

3 Think of three new words that start with each of these prefixes. Don't use the examples already given in the table on the previous page!

a) trans– _______ _______ _______
b) ir– _______ _______ _______
c) mid– _______ _______ _______
d) inter– _______ _______ _______
e) anti– _______ _______ _______

(3 marks each) /15

4 Put the correct word on the line to complete each sentence.

a) The decorators _______ the old house into a modern habitation.
(transformed informed reformed disformed uniformed)

b) Andy thought the cakes were _______.
(resistable irrespective irresistible unresistible inresistible)

(1 mark each) /2

5 Use your knowledge of prefixes to explain these words.

a) antifreeze _______
b) forenoon _______
c) hypermarket _______
d) semi-detached _______
e) midland _______
f) irresponsible _______
g) co-star _______
h) post-war _______

(1 mark each) /8

CHALLENGE Make a prefix table using these prefixes:
ante– counter– under– aut(o)– mal– mon(o)–

Suffixes

Definition: A suffix is a group of letters placed at the end of a word. The suffix changes the meaning of the word.
Knowing suffixes can make spelling easier and increase your vocabulary.
Beware – some suffixes change the spelling of the word!

Examples:

Suffix	Makes	Meaning	Example
–acy	noun	state of being	piracy
–ist		one who does	pianist
–dom		place or state	kingdom
–ess		female	actress
–tion / –sion		state of being	extension
–ster		person	mobster
–ness		state of being	friendliness
–ize / –ise	verb	to make or become	liquidise
–ish	adjective	have the quality of	foolish
–ic / –ac		like / pertaining to	aquatic
–ous		having / full of	delicious

Let's practise!

Match the suffixes and the words to make the words mean a state of being. Change the word spelling if necessary.

Suffixes: –acy –dom –tion –sion –ness
Words: diplomat elated sad free

1. Read the question, then read it again. What are you being asked to do? — **Make the words mean a state of being.**
2. Look at the first word and think of it as a state of being. — **diplomat – you would be in a state of diplomacy.**
3. Look at the next word. — **elated – you would be full of elation.**
4. Look at the next word. — **sad – you would be full of sadness.**
5. Look at the last word. — **free – you would be in a state of freedom.**

TOP TIP

When you learn suffixes, their spellings and meanings, link them to learning the etymology (origin) of words. Since lots of words use the same suffixes, you learn new words and spellings in one go.

TOP TIP

Now try these questions:

1 Remove the suffixes and write the root words correctly.

a) satisfaction ______ **b)** artist ______ **c)** gangster ______
d) friendship ______ **e)** adventurous ______ **f)** goddess ______

2 Circle the four words that would go with the suffix to make new words.

a) –ish child new cost fool sweet
b) –tion collect decorate rotate direct fate
c) –ist dental piano record chemistry science
d) –ness great sick sweet think thick

3 Think of three different words that end with each of these suffixes.

a) –sion ______ ______ ______
b) –ous ______ ______ ______
c) –ise ______ ______ ______
d) –ic ______ ______ ______
e) –ess ______ ______ ______

4 Put the missing word on the line to complete each sentence correctly.

a) The model looked very ______ .
(realicist / realistic / realist / realic)

b) Her ______ is important to the Queen.
(private / privately / privacy / privateness)

c) The ______ on the motorway caused a lot of damage.
(collision / collition / colliding / collidiment)

5 Write the meaning of each word.

a) cellist ______
b) stylish ______
c) rotation ______
d) forgiveness ______
e) televise ______
f) princess ______

CHALLENGE Find as many suffixes as you can on one page of a reading book and then research their meanings.

Achieved? ☺ 😐 ☹

(1 mark each) /6

(4 marks for each line) /16

(3 marks for each line) /15

(1 mark for each line) /3

(1 mark for each line) /6

Plurals

A quick revision! **Irregular plurals:**

Ending in	To form the plural	Example	Exceptions
ch, x, s, sh	add –es	watches	
o	add –es	volcanoes	words of Spanish and Italian origin, tacos
y	drop the y and add –ies	cities	words ending in –ey, e.g. donkeys
is	change the i to e	crises	
us	drop the us and add i	stimuli	
f	drop the f and add ves	loaves	e.g. chefs, beliefs

Other irregular plurals: These do not follow the usual patterns. Examples:

child – children   person – people   man – men   woman – women
ox – oxen   foot – feet   goose – geese   mouse – mice   tooth – teeth

Zero plurals: These plurals are exactly the same as the singular noun. Examples:

aircraft   fish   headquarters   sheep   species
deer   moose   crossroads   salmon   barracks   pike

Let's practise!

Use **aircraft** in a sentence that shows it is singular and then in a different sentence that shows it is plural.

1	Read the question, then read it again. What are you being asked to do?	**Write two sentences, one showing aircraft as a singular noun and one showing it as a plural.**
2	Think about the singular.	**That means there is one aircraft.**
3	Write a sentence about one aircraft.	**The aircraft is approaching the runway.**
4	Think about the plural.	**That means there are two or more aircraft.**
5	Write a sentence about more than one aircraft.	**The aircraft were circling above the airport, queuing for the landing strip.**
6	Write your answers.	**The aircraft is approaching the runway. The aircraft were circling above the airport, queuing for the landing strip.**

Now try these questions:

Achieved? ☺ 😐 ☹

1 Write the plural of these nouns.

a) ditch ____________ **b)** hoax ____________
c) lorry ____________ **d)** leaf ____________
e) counter ____________ **f)** piano ____________
g) gas ____________ **h)** potato ____________

(1 mark each) /8

2 Write the plural of these irregular nouns.

a) man ____________ **b)** foot ____________
c) person ____________ **d)** appendix ____________
e) mouse ____________ **f)** this ____________
g) ox ____________ **h)** fungus ____________

(1 mark each) /8

3 Circle the nouns that are zero plurals.

tadpole	fleece	moose	jubilee	spaghetti	headquarters
office	cooker	tuna	carpet	network	bison

(1 mark for each correct one) /5

4 Use these zero plurals in two sentences each. In one sentence use them as a singular noun and in the other as a plural noun.

a) crossroads ____________

b) sheep ____________

c) furniture ____________

d) species ____________

(1 mark for each sentence) /8

CHALLENGE Use the Internet and dictionaries to list all the irregular and zero plurals you can find.

Homophones and similar words

Some words are often used incorrectly, even by adults. Learn how to use them and you are getting ahead of the game!

Similar words that end in ce and se:
advice / advise   device / devise   practice / practise   licence / license

The words ending in ce are nouns
(imagine changing the c to an a and then you know it is **a thing**):
a piece of advice   a practice   a device   a licence

The words ending in se are verbs.
(imagine the s as a wriggly letter and you know it is **doing** something)
to advise   to devise   to practise   to license

Let's practise!

Put the words prophesy and prophecy in the correct places in this sentence.

When the man started to __________ , he made a __________ that affected everyone.

1	Read the question, then read it again. What are you being asked to do?	**Put the words correctly in the sentence.**
2	Think what type of word is needed in the first space.	**started to ______ He was doing something so we need a verb.**
3	Check which of the words is a verb.	**The word with s is the verb (it's a wriggly letter!) so he started to prophesy.**
4	Think what type of word is needed in the second space.	**made a ______ He made something so we need a noun.**
5	Check which of the words is a noun.	**The word with c is the noun (change the c to a) so he made a prophecy.**
6	Write the complete sentence.	**When the man started to prophesy, he made a prophecy that affected everyone.**

TOP TIP

Use these clues to remember these words:
stationary – not moving (think of not getting away from point **a**)
stationery – papers, envelopes, etc. (**e** for envelopes and easy to write)

TOP TIP

Now try this question:

1 Use these words in sentences to illustrate their meaning. Check in a dictionary first if you need to.

a) affect ______
effect ______

b) aloud ______
allowed ______

c) farther ______
father ______

d) altar ______
alter ______

e) compliment ______
complement ______

f) profit ______
prophet ______

g) whose ______
who's ______

h) advice ______
advise ______

i) past ______
passed ______

j) cereal ______
serial ______

k) principal ______
principle ______

Achieved? ☺ 😐 ☹

(1 mark for each pair)

/11

CHALLENGE

Find other pairs of words that are commonly used incorrectly and write them with their definitions.

Synonyms and antonyms

Definitions: Synonyms are words that have the same (or a similar) meaning.
Antonyms are words that have opposite meanings.
Finding synonyms and antonyms is not only fun, but it also increases your vocabulary.

Examples:

Word	Synonym	Antonym
wisdom	intelligence	foolishness
endure	withstand	capitulate
solemn	serious	joyous
reveal	uncover	conceal
frail	weak	robust
hopeful	optimistic	hopeless
natural	genuine	artificial
hindrance	impediment	help

Let's practise!

Fill the blanks in this sentence with a pair of antonyms.

It took 80 years to ____________ the cathedral and a few minutes to ____________ it.

1	Read the question, then read it again. What are you being asked to do?	**Find a pair of antonyms that will complete the sentence.**
2	Think about what information the sentence contains.	**It tells you that something took a long time and the opposite happened very quickly.**
3	Consider an antonym pair that might fit.	**Find / lose – no, if it took 80 years to find the cathedral, how could you lose it? Build – it could take 80 years to build a cathedral. An antonym of build is demolish. You could demolish a cathedral in minutes if you blew it up.**
4	Write the complete sentence.	**It took 80 years to build the cathedral and a few minutes to demolish it.**

TOP TIP

Learning new words and their meanings helps to build an effective, rich vocabulary. The more you know, the better you can communicate. Look up synonym and antonym games on the Internet to help you learn more quickly.

TOP TIP

Now try these questions:

Achieved? ☺ 😐 ☹

1 Underline the odd word out in each list of synonyms.

a) terminate, commence, start, originate
b) sympathy, compassion, commission, care
c) lenient, tolerant, easy-going, determined
d) wilt, wither, abundance, shrivel
e) fantastic, atrocious, marvellous, brilliant

(1 mark each) /5

2 Highlight a synonym and underline an antonym for each word.

a) cautious — confident conscious wary weary
b) jealous — extensive envious content contentious
c) success — failure uncertainty triumph abrupt

(1 mark for each line) /3

3 Write a pair of antonyms to complete each sentence.

a) We will have to ____________ more flour if we want to make more cakes to ____________ .

b) We came in through the main ____________ and left through the fire ____________ .

(1 mark for each line) /2

4 Write an antonym of each word and then write a sentence containing both words.

a) export ____________________

____

b) departure ____________________

____

c) overweight ____________________

____

d) interior ____________________

____

e) victory ____________________

____

f) insult ____________________

____

(2 marks each) /12

CHALLENGE Use a thesaurus to find some words with at least four syllables, and write a synonym for each.

Figurative language

Purpose: Using figurative language makes your writing more expressive and interesting. It also extends your ability to use language to communicate.

Types of figurative language:

Simile This says something is like something else. The fire was as hot as the sun. 	**Onomatopoeia** A word that makes the sound it describes. The paper rustled. 'Pop!' went the balloon. 
Metaphor This says something is something else. The fire was the sun, blazing through the night. 	**Personification** A special type of metaphor that gives an object human characteristics. The window winked at me. 

Let's practise!

Complete the sentence using each of the different types of figurative language shown.

The door		(simile)
		(metaphor)
		(personification)
		(onomatopoeia)

1. Read the question, then read it again. What are you being asked to do?
   Use figurative language to put endings on the sentence.
2. Think of a simile. Use the words as or like.
   The door was as solid as a rock.
3. Think of a metaphor.
   The door is a dragon, guarding the exit.
4. Think of some personification.
   The door begged me to enter the room.
5. Think of an onomatopoeia word for what a door does.
   The door banged shut.
6. Write your answer in the table.

The door	was as solid as a rock.	(simile)
	is a dragon, guarding the exit.	(metaphor)
	begged me to enter the room.	(personification)
	banged shut.	(onomatopoeia)

Now try these questions.

Achieved? ☺ 😐 ☹

1 Join each phrase or clause to the type of figurative language it illustrates. *(1 mark each)* /6

as high as a kite | the car screamed | the girl mumbled

simile | metaphor | personification | onomatopoeia

the fog was a grey blanket | the crisps crunched | flew like a bird

2 Complete these similes: *(1 mark each)* /10

a) as tall as ____________	**b)** as white as ____________
c) as wise as ____________	**d)** as hungry as ____________
e) as brave as ____________	**f)** as proud as ____________
g) as deaf as ____________	**h)** as blind as ____________
i) as busy as ____________	**j)** as slippery as ____________

3 Write the onomatopoeia words for the noise made by: *(1 mark each)* /6

a) a clock ____________	**b)** a plate breaking ____________
c) a bee ____________	**d)** a light switch ____________
e) sausages cooking ____________	**f)** a duck ____________

4 Complete each sentence using the different types of figurative language shown. *(1 mark each)* /12

The bus	(simile)
	(metaphor)
	(personification)
	(onomatopoeia)
The flowers	(simile)
	(metaphor)
	(personification)
	(onomatopoeia)
The wind	(simile)
	(metaphor)
	(personification)
	(onomatopoeia)

CHALLENGE Find examples of figurative language and explain why the author used them and why they are effective.

Idioms

Definition: Groups of words that do not mean exactly what they say!
Purpose: To convey meaning in a more colourful way.
Uses: In speech and informal writing.

Let's practise!

Underline the idiom and draw an arrow to the picture that shows what it means.

I'm feeling under the weather.

1	Read the question, then read it again. What are you being asked to do?	Find the idiom in the sentence and show what it means.
2	Look for the words in the sentence that you wouldn't really do or see.	I'm feeling – that makes sense. under the weather – how can you be under the weather?
3	Underline those words.	under the weather.
4	Now think about or find out what the idiom means and join it to the correct meaning.	Under the weather means feeling ill. I'm feeling under the weather.

TOP TIP Try to learn some new idioms – the more you know, the more chance you have to use them. **TOP TIP**

TOP TIP If people use idioms that you don't understand, ask them to explain them. That way you learn more! Here are two more idioms to learn: **TOP TIP**

Chew the fat (means gossip or idle chat)

Hit the sack (means go to bed)

Now try these questions:

Achieved? ☺ 😐 ☹

1 Underline the idioms in these sentences and explain what they mean.

a) If you lend a hand we can do it easily.

b) It was raining cats and dogs.

c) We were told to jump to it.

d) The tickets cost an arm and a leg.

e) We were racing against the clock to beat the other team.

(1 mark each) /5

2 Use these idioms to write sentences that show what they mean. The first one has been done for you.

a) no room to swing a cat

The house was so small there was no room to swing a cat!

b) over the top

c) pipe down

d) tongue in cheek

e) the last straw

(1 mark each) /4

3 Find and write an idiom that means:

the family bond is stronger than anything else

(1 mark) /1

CHALLENGE

Find and make a list of ten interesting idioms to use in your writing. You could try searching on the Internet.

Etymology

Definition: Etymology is the study of the origins of words. It looks at where words came from and how they have changed over time.

Etymology is fascinating and helps you to build and understand vocabulary. A good dictionary will tell you the origin of a word as well as its meaning today.

The words we use today have come from lots of different languages, although many of our words come from Greek and Latin.

Let's practise!

For each of these word roots, write two modern words that are related to the root.

Word root	Origin	Meaning	Examples
mobilis	Latin	moveable	
astron	Greek	a star	

1 Read the question, then read it again. What are you being asked to do?

Find words that relate to the word root that is given.

2 Study the first word root.

***mobilis*, which means moveable, so we need words that look similar and are to do with moving.**

3 Select words that are related.

mobile, mobility, immobile

4 Study the second word root.

***astron*, which means a star, so we need words that look similar and are to do with stars.**

5 Select words that are related.

astronomy, astrology, astronaut

6 Complete the table.

Word root	Origin	Meaning	Examples
mobilis	Latin	moveable	mobile, mobility, immobile
astron	Greek	a star	astronomy, astrology, astronaut

TOP TIP

Find a dictionary that tells you the etymology of words. Whenever you look up a word, check the etymology and use it to help you remember and understand the word.

TOP TIP

Now try these questions:

Achieved? ☺ 😐 ☹

1 Match the word with its etymology.

Word	Etymology
alarm	Chinese – *ke-tsiap* was a sauce invented at the end of the 17th century.
ketchup	Italian – means 'To arms!'
robot	French – means 'good air'. In the Middle Ages if you smelled good you were thought to be healthier and happier.
bungalow	Old German – *hus* means 'house' and *bunda* means 'owner'. A homeowner would be a good person to marry!
debonair	Hindi – means 'one-storey house'.
husband	Latin – *liber* means 'to peel' and would refer to the inner bark of a tree that manuscripts were written on.
library	Italian – small ball or pebble that was used to cast a vote in a box.
ballot	Czech – means 'worker'.
salary	Latin – Roman soldiers were paid a handful of salt a day, which was replaced by money as it was easier to transport, so soldiers got their salt money (*salarium*).
sinister	Old English – *stol* meant 'throne'.
stool	Old French – means 'cooked twice'.
biscuit	Latin for 'left'; the left side was thought to be evil.

(1 mark each) /12

2 For each of these word roots, write two modern words that are related to the origin.

Word root	Origin	Meaning	Examples
aqua	Latin	water	
autos	Greek	self	
globus	Latin	sphere	
mikros	Greek	small	

(1 mark each) /4

3 For each of these word roots, use the modern words to deduce (work out) the meaning of the root.

Word root	Origin	Meaning	Examples
solus	Latin		desolate, sole, solo, solipsism
mortis	Latin		mortal, mortuary, immortal, mortality
bios	Greek		biography, biology, biosphere, biologist

(1 mark each) /3

CHALLENGE

Use the Internet and an etymological dictionary to see how many languages you can find that have words we use or have adapted for the English language.

Spelling word list for Years 5 and 6

accommodate
accompany
according
achieve
aggressive
amateur
ancient
apparent
appreciate
attached
available
average
awkward
bargain
bruise
category
cemetery
committee
communicate
community
competition
conscience*
conscious*
controversy
convenience
correspond
criticise (critic + ise)
curiosity
definite
desperate
determined
develop
dictionary
disastrous
embarrass
environment
equip (–ped, –ment)
especially
exaggerate
excellent
existence
explanation
familiar
foreign
forty
frequently
government
guarantee
harass
hindrance
identity
immediate(ly)
individual
interfere
interrupt
language
leisure
lightning
marvellous
mischievous
muscle
necessary
neighbour
nuisance
occupy
occur
opportunity
parliament
persuade
physical
prejudice
privilege
profession
programme
pronunciation
queue
recognise
recommend
relevant
restaurant
rhyme
rhythm
sacrifice
secretary
shoulder
sincere(ly)
soldier
stomach
sufficient
suggest
symbol
system
temperature
thorough
twelfth
variety
vegetable
vehicle
yacht

Many of these words can be used for practice in adding suffixes.

*Conscience and conscious are related to science – all come from the Latin word meaning 'to know'. Conscience is simply science with the prefix con– added. Conscious also contains the 'sci' of science.